"Lisa Miller's story is true, tough, and told with tenderness. *Only One Mommy* deals sensitively with a difficult subject that Christians would rather avoid, but is being thrust upon us."

Wendy Wright
President of Concerned Women for America
Washington, DC

"*Only One Mommy* is worth the price of three books. It is the tragic story of a woman, Lisa Miller, whose family dysfunction and abuse in childhood led her into multiple addictions—including homosexuality. It is a warning about a legal system designed to protect the rights of a natural parent, which is now being used to abuse those rights, and more broadly about a political movement bent on stifling the exercise of religious liberty for all. And, thirdly, it is the touching story of how the author, Rena Lindevaldsen, came to realize that what Lisa really needed was a Christian woman who would be her friend, not just her lawyer. Every citizen who cares about freedom, every parent, every person struggling with same-sex attractions, and every Christian who wants to minister to them should read this book."

Peter Sprigg
Senior Fellow for Policy Studies
Family Research Council
Washington, DC

D1314346

The Lisa Miller Story

Only One Mommy

A Woman's Battle for
Her Life, Her Daughter,
and Her Freedom

Rena M. Lindevaldsen, Esq.

New
Revolution
Publishers

The Lisa Miller Story

Only One Mommy

By Rena M. Lindevaldsen, Esq.

ISBN: 978-1-937102-01-2   Paperback

Published by:

New Revolution Publishers™
P.O. Box 540774
Orlando, Florida 32854
www.NewRevolutionPublishers.com
(800) 671-1776

Cover and Interior Design by:
Heather Kirk
www.GraphicsByHeather.com

Cover Photo of Mother & Child
and **Input on Cover Design:**
Hannah Reichel

Dedication

To Lisa Miller for entrusting her life story to me; my husband and family for their unfailing support, encouragement, and sacrifice; Mat & Anita Staver for their inspiration and leadership; my friends at Liberty Counsel, Liberty University School of Law, and Thomas Road Baptist Church for their steadfast support; and all those in the pro-family movement who allow me to serve alongside them in this battle to preserve God's design for marriage and family.

Contents

Introduction

"How many moms do you have?" This is a question most of us have never asked, or heard asked, but even the youngest child knows the answer: only one mommy. Unfortunately, with each passing day, the answer is becoming less obvious due to the efforts of people who are tirelessly working to destroy the mother-father family paradigm and replace it with a subjective, ever-changing definition of family that could include two moms, two dads, two moms and a dad, or any other combination — courts and legislatures across the country already are actively redefining families in this way. The impact of this radical shift reaches far beyond issues confronting same-sex couples: government is increasingly exercising control over all families concerning matters that long have been within the exclusive control of parents.

For example, if you are a single mom with a live-in boyfriend for a few years, or even a few months, when you end the relationship, a court can decide that your child formed an attachment to your former boyfriend so that he is now entitled to visitation (or custody) over your objections. Parents who homeschool their children are finding courts ordering them to send their children to public schools because the court believes it is harmful for the children to be excluded from the public school environment. Parents with children in public schools already have discovered that they have no say in what the schools teach their children about sexuality or religion. Without parental consent or knowledge, courts have held that schools can, and should, read to elementary students a book about a prince who marries a man in order to teach children that all family structures are the same. Armed with broad discretion to decide "what is in the best interests of a child," courts are stripping parents of their God-given right and obligation to raise their children. That is exactly what courts have done to Lisa Miller.

Lisa Miller, and her biological daughter, Isabella, have been embroiled in an interstate custody dispute for more than seven years because a Vermont court declared the factually impossible — that Isabella has two mommies. Lisa repeatedly was ordered to treat her former same-sex partner as Isabella's second mother or face loss of custody and jail time. In fall 2009, Lisa unexpectedly disappeared with her daughter.

During the years of ongoing litigation, God not only transformed Lisa's life, taking her out of the homosexual lifestyle, He has used her to counsel other women struggling with addictions, including homosexuality. She also became the face of the battle to redefine family in this Nation. Her story has been told in the *Washington Post Magazine* and *Newsweek*, on CNN, and ABC Nightline, and on radio programs around the country. In a testimony I heard her give in 2008, Lisa explained that through the years of litigation:

> "I have grown closer to Him through my trials. I have come to Him with a broken and contrite spirit and He has given me rest and peace. I know that He will not give me any more than I can handle. God has turned my stubborn spirit and the grief of my past into a joy of my salvation. It has been a joy to walk with Him. My trials have given me opportunities to share Christ. I believe that my past can be used to help others and that God can use my past-repented sin for His glory and honor."

Lisa is always the first to admit that she made many mistakes in her life, even having a child out of wedlock because *she* wanted a child. Once God got a hold of her life, however, she knew she had an obligation to raise her child according to the Bible. She took very seriously the admonition in *Proverbs 22:6*: "Train a child in the way he should go, and when he is old he will not turn from it." Lisa considered it a direct conflict with her Biblical obligations as a parent to turn her child over to someone who was not Isabella's parent and was actively engaged in the homosexual lifestyle. Turning from the Christian foundations of this Nation, our courts disagreed with Lisa and ordered her to turn her child over to her former same-sex partner.

This book is for every American who cherishes God's word and the Christian heritage of this country and who values liberty. This book is for those who know someone caught in the homosexual lifestyle and wonder, "How did it happen?" "What can I do?" "How can I help?" It's for pastors and leaders who understand the need to start ministries that embrace those struggling with homosexuality in order to show them that they can choose to leave homosexuality through the saving grace of Jesus Christ. This book is for anyone struggling with homosexuality or other addictions, and wanting to hear one woman's story about how she got involved in the addictions and how she overcame them through a moment-by-moment dependence on her Savior. Finally, this book is for anyone considering the option of starting a family with a same-sex partner. Even if you have no desire to leave homosexuality, this book is for you because you need to know the legal (as well as emotional and spiritual) consequences of your decision to have a child with your partner.

A Note About the Author and the Information Contained in the Book

The personal information about Lisa Miller's life contained in this book comes first-hand from Lisa Miller. Because I was not able to consult with Lisa after fall 2009, there are undoubtedly some sections where Lisa could have filled in more details. I believe, however, that in the pages that follow the message of hope and healing for all who desire something more for their life comes through.

I first encountered Lisa in June 2004, when Liberty Counsel received a phone call from a woman who said that she was a former homosexual trying to prevent her ex-partner from getting custody of her daughter. At the time, Liberty Counsel had never handled such a case, nor had I. In fact, there was no case law whatsoever dealing with the unique issues involved in multi-state litigation of a custody order arising out of a same-sex relationship. When we realized the sincerity of Lisa's desire to raise her child according to the truths of Scripture and discovered the direct attack on parental rights that had been waged by the Vermont courts, we agreed to help. Nearly seven years later,

I've been involved in litigation in defense of parental rights and traditional marriage in fifteen states. I've watched the judiciary strip parents of their rights and call marriage between one man and one woman bigoted, discriminatory, and lacking any rational basis. I've wept with moms who face losing their children to former same-sex partners and realize the mistake they made in choosing the homosexual lifestyle but who earnestly desire to protect their children from that lifestyle. I've listened to angry parents who cannot understand why schools are teaching our young children that it is normal and healthy to engage in sexual activity (both same-sex and opposite-sex) at an early age. I've also read thousands of pages of literature and court documents in which it is clear that there are groups in America who desire to destroy God's design for family and strip citizens of their God-given, constitutionally guaranteed religious liberties.

As a result of her personal struggle with addictions, including homosexuality, and the legal struggle to preserve her parental rights, Lisa and I want to get a much-needed message out to churches and to the majority of Americans who desire to preserve the Christian principles upon which our Nation was founded. Our desire for this book is that it encourages churches and individual Christians to begin in earnest to minister to those in the homosexual lifestyle, that it serves as a wake-up call for all Americans to realize that the culture war is taking place in their own backyards, and that it gives hope and encouragement to those who want to leave the homosexual lifestyle.

Chapter One

Lisa's Childhood Years

Lisa was born on September 6, 1968. Her mother often reminded Lisa that her birth was unplanned. "Whenever my mother was mad at me, she would pull out the oval peach colored pack of birth control pills that she had saved all those years to show me that only one week was missing, and that was the week she got pregnant." Her brother, who was born three and a half years earlier, also knew that he was unplanned.

Lisa was a sickly baby, weighing only 5 lbs 2 oz. The delivery was hard on her mother, leaving her on bed rest for two weeks. "It seemed as if she didn't want me or care for me from conception. I'm told that my mother refused to even hold me as a baby. My aunt had to come take care of me for the first two months of my life." Like many young children, whenever she heard an argument between her parents, she would tell herself it was her fault; she wondered whether her parents' marriage would be better if she hadn't been born.

Lisa's parents divorced when she was seven, which only added to her insecurity. Both children initially stayed with their mother and, for a while, were not allowed to visit their dad. The next several years ushered in consistent communication that Lisa was a mistake and failure. School reinforced this idea, as Lisa struggled academically and was a loner. As she thinks back on her time with her mother, she realizes that there was no mother-child bond. "I do not remember my mother telling me I was pretty or smart. I do not remember my mother ever telling me it was okay to fail. Even when I was young, I don't remember my mother spending time with me — sitting on the floor to play games as I do with my daughter, teaching me how to cook or even helping me pick out my clothes for school." Lisa found herself wanting to become invisible. Seeking a way to escape reality, Lisa became an avid reader:

> "Once a week, my mom would take my brother and me to the library. Once there, we were free to stay in the children's section and take out the maximum number of books — 50! I carefully chose 50 books each week because they had to last me the entire week. I read all 50 books each week. When I grew older, the library became my source of comfort because I could get lost between the pages of a book. Even today, I enjoy the peace and quiet of a good book."

Another source of comfort, although difficult to call it that, was the ability to be in control of something in her life. At age six, just a year before her parents' divorce, Lisa dabbled for the first time in controlling her life through food. She had been sick for a few days, vomiting, and not able to keep anything in her stomach. In her home, being sick meant she was no longer invisible, which meant that she was an added burden to her mother. "When I was sick, I was punished rather than taken care of. It was common practice to hear 'Make sure you throw up in the bathroom so you don't get your room dirty.' I do not remember a kind word or a cool rag on my forehead or even an 'I am sorry you are sick, I wish I could make it better.'" So, when she began to feel better, she refused to eat so that she could be certain not to get sick again. She liked the sense of finally being in control of something in her life. Eventually, Lisa was admitted to the hospital where they fed her intravenously for four days. "Even though I was very ill and lethargic, I liked being in the hospital. People from my church came to visit me. I got presents and get well cards. I also was out of the house and could do nothing all day that could get me into trouble." This was the beginning of her first addiction — controlling food intake as a means of bringing order to her chaotic life; it later became a full-fledged eating disorder.

Lisa's mother's behavior grew more erratic after the divorce and she turned to Lisa for emotional and physical support. Her mother had just "shut down." It wasn't until years later that Lisa learned that her mother suffered from untreated mental health issues. "The house became a mess. Dinner was rarely prepared. I never knew what to expect when she was at home. It felt as though I had become the mom and she had become the child. She couldn't even sleep by herself and eventually moved into my bedroom."

For the first year after her parents separated, Lisa wasn't permitted to see her father. Even after she began visiting her father, for years Lisa wasn't permitted to go anywhere else except school and church. She wasn't even permitted to participate in any after school activity or attend birthday parties:

> "I was a latch key kid and if mom didn't pick me up from after school care then I was allowed to walk home and use my key to let myself in the empty house. I didn't like coming home to an empty house. I had nightmares of a witch coming to get me and I was always afraid that the witch was in the house. On the other hand, I was grateful that the house was empty because when my mom was home I lived in fear; I did not know what mood my mom would be in when she finally got home. Most nights she was home around 8:00 p.m. and she was mad about something at work. Often she would bring home with her the legal briefs she was typing for work and make me read them. The briefs were pretty sickening, outlining sexual crimes and murder plots. It was during these years that I became quiet on the outside but wild on the inside."

After Lisa's mother stopped attending church, she allowed Lisa to continue. Since it was the only time, other than school, that Lisa was allowed to leave the house, she attended regularly. "I loved sitting there and having no one bother me. I enjoyed the challenge of learning verses and it became my secret game to figure out who I could beat. Although I did poorly at school, at church I could be somebody and I tried my best to win every competition. Little did I know that I was 'hiding God's word in my heart' and that all the memorization would come back to me almost 25 years later!"

In the second or third grade, Lisa tried her mother's diet candy, which was kept in the freezer. She loved the way it made her feel, almost like she "was on the top of the world," after which she would eventually drift off to sleep. Since she didn't want her mother to notice the candy was slowly disappearing, Lisa began purchasing diet pills at the local drugstore. When the diet pills did not make her sleepy, as the diet candy had, she bought sleeping pills as well. The pharmacist let her purchase the pills because she told him they were for her mother. This was the beginning of Lisa's second addiction. "I didn't know the diet pills were speed until four years later when I entered the sixth grade and was caught with them in my purse. All I knew was that I was a different person when I took them. I also liked the way I felt when I ate the diet candy and popped the diet pills — nothing at all seemed to bother me." The pills also helped cover the pain of the emotional and physical abuse that occurred at the hands of her mother:

> "It was during this first year of separation that my mom started abusing me — or at least that is when I first remember it happening. She would go outside and cut a switch from the rose bush and use that to hit me. I never knew it was coming. I never knew what to expect. My mom became adept at ensuring that all marks she inflicted on me were beneath the clothes so no one would know."

Thankfully, along the years, God provided Lisa with caring teachers in school and at church. She remembers her third and fourth grade Sunday school teacher who sent a weekly post card with a sticker about God's love on it and encouraged Lisa to memorize Bible verses. Above all, the teacher took the time to set expectations for her students; she showed Lisa consistency for the first time in her life, took the time to show her students that she cared about them, and instilled in Lisa the idea that she could accomplish something. At the end of the year, Lisa received a certificate for memorizing the most Bible verses. The certificate meant so much to Lisa that she kept it through her adulthood. Although they lost touch over the years, "today, by the grace of God, I am in contact with her. She read an article about my legal case in a newspaper and sent me an e-mail through the author who wrote the story. She still sends me encouraging thoughts and, yes, she still teaches Sunday school. I love it when she sends me what she thinks the Lord wants me to know. It is always timely and much needed." The other positive by-product of this teacher's encouraging Lisa to memorize Bible verses was that Lisa's mother usually left her alone if Lisa said she was working on her Sunday school lesson.

By the time she entered fifth grade, Lisa's pill addiction wasn't enough to control the feelings of chaos, loneliness, and hopelessness. "I needed something else to keep my mind off my life and to feel in control, so I began starving and binging. I took careful notes in a journal on how much I ate, what I ate, and when I ate. I took detailed notes on what I needed to do differently to control side effects of headaches from not eating and a burning throat from self-induced vomiting." In the sixth grade, it became apparent that something was wrong with Lisa. She was falling asleep in class and hanging out with "the bad crowd." Her sixth grade teacher learned that Lisa was taking diet pills and explained to her that the pills were "speed." Lisa's teacher encouraged her to make changes in her life, including hanging out with a new set of friends. Scared, Lisa lied and told the teacher that she was taking the pills to help her lose weight — not as a way to escape from the realities of life.

Concerned for Lisa, the teacher created a "biggest loser" game for the students: the student who lost the most weight through proper diet and exercise would be taken out to dinner by the other students. Unfortunately, the teacher called Lisa's mother about the pills, who then searched Lisa's purse and room. She found boxes of sleeping pills and diet pills, as well as the journals. She punished Lisa for "making her look bad," but nevertheless gave Lisa permission to participate in the competition. Lisa put aside the pills, exercised, and won the competition. In essence, the competition channeled Lisa's need for control and stability away from diet pills and eating disorders to proper eating and exercise. Unfortunately, after the competition was over, Lisa returned to the pills and eating disorders as a means of escaping reality and feeling in control again. No one suspected because she hid the pills in new places, burned her old journals, and learned to commit to memory all the details of her strict eating and pill regimen. The teacher's small act of kindness, however, stayed with Lisa through adulthood. She even remembers the name of the restaurant — Joe Theismann's.

That sixth grade year also was when Lisa began her third addiction — smoking. The same friends her sixth grade teacher warned her to stay away from skipped school to go smoke. Lisa "was too chicken to skip school" but would meet up with them after school. It was relatively easy for Lisa to get cigarettes because her father owned a country store and she worked there on the weekends she visited him. When her dad left her alone, Lisa would steal cigarettes. After a while, her dad realized someone was stealing from him. "He threatened that if he found out who was taking the cigarettes he would make that person eat the entire pack in front of him. By now, I knew he was serious and I was not about to get caught. I immediately quit smoking."

Sixth grade was also memorable because it was the year that Lisa's brother went to live with their dad. After that, Lisa only saw her brother during weekend visits. At this time, Lisa's mother planted the seeds for Lisa's next addiction — pornography. Lisa's mother began to buy pornographic magazines so she could tear out pictures of the women and tape them to the wall. She would make Lisa look at the pictures and warn her never to be like those women, that men were no good, and that men only wanted one thing from women. Lisa wondered what they were doing in the pictures so she taught herself about the "birds and the bees" by reading an entire set of child development books that were on her mother's bookshelf. The pictures her mother put up were different than the books though. "My mother would display the pictures and talk about what they were doing. She said she wanted to make sure that I didn't turn out like those women, but she began to obsess about sex. Because of the reading I had done, when my mother began taping the pictures on the wall upstairs, I just studied them more. Pornography is powerful; I was lured into that world." At the age of 40, she still remembered the very first picture her mother put on the wall.

With her interest piqued, Lisa began to read "naughty books." As a teenager, she was given access to all the books in the public library, not just the children's section. At first, she filled her book bag with romance novels. Later, she graduated to adult novels that "would make the average person blush. I became addicted to reading about sex and looking at the pictures in my mother's magazines."

In the meantime, in the eighth grade, Lisa's mother put her in a Christian school where she learned even more about the Bible than she had in Sunday school. She explained that,

> "my eighth grade teacher was very young and conservative. She believed that girls should learn those skills needed in order to become a better wife; she would take us to her apartment to teach us to sew and cook as part of her class. We also memorized entire chapters of the Bible and learned about the doctrines of the world. It was at this school that I learned about creation and evolution. I became a staunch supporter of creationism, reading books on evolution so I could debate how creationism was superior to the theory of evolution. I remember debating the hot topics of the news hour with my dad on the long car ride to his store. I liked debating because it made me feel in control."

That small element of control became especially important during Lisa's high school years because her mother's behavior became more erratic.

In the ninth grade, Lisa transferred to a different school. The drastic differences between the two schools only fueled Lisa's sense of insecurity and chaos. The school was much bigger than the last and didn't require uniforms. Lisa felt insecure about her old and outdated clothing. When she complained about it at home, it just made life more miserable. By this point, Lisa's mother was delusional. Lisa remembers one night when her mother came into Lisa's room in the middle of the night, knife in hand, telling Lisa that she would have to kill her because she was the devil. Sadly, this wasn't the first time something like this happened, so Lisa knew how to talk her "down" out of the delusion.

About this time, Lisa tried to reach out for help. She told a senior leader in her church what was happening at home. He didn't believe her, though, in essence telling her that she was making it up. He kept telling Lisa it couldn't be true because her mother was a good Christian who had taught Sunday school for years in the church. He didn't realize, however, how ill Lisa's mother was and that what people act like in public isn't always how they act at home. Lisa never directly reached out for help again; instead, she tried to find new ways to cope with the physical and emotional abuse that she lived with at home. She continued to take pills and to alternate between starving herself and binging. When this wasn't enough to control the pain and emptiness, because she could only get pills when she managed to steal money from her mother, she tried to end her life. She remembers,

> "I didn't know what else to do so one day I picked up a razor blade to kill myself. I was too chicken to go through with it but discovered that I liked the feeling I got after cutting myself. I know now that that feeling is euphoria because when someone cuts themselves, endorphins are automatically released into the system, which in turn eases physical pain and circumvents emotional pain. I was hooked. I cut on a regular basis — well into adulthood. It was easy and no one knew because I was always careful to cut in those places that were hidden beneath my clothes."

Lisa spent much of her ninth grade year as a loner — until a new student enrolled. She developed a friendship with Lisa that lasted into their adulthood. What made the friendship so special was that she accepted Lisa for who she was, where she was, and didn't judge her by ostracizing her because of the life she lived. The two of them began writing anonymous letters to one of their teachers, telling the teacher what was going on in their lives. To her credit, the teacher eventually figured out who was writing the letters, but didn't expressly tell the girls she knew. Instead, throughout that summer, she organized several sightseeing trips for the girls to attend with her. "Amazingly, my mom allowed me to go with her."

During tenth grade, this same teacher decided to mentor and counsel Lisa. Although she didn't have a degree in counseling, she wanted to help a young girl she knew was hurting. For the first month, Lisa resisted the counseling, refusing to say anything at all about her life. In fact, Lisa wouldn't even look at the teacher during their counseling sessions. Eventually, Lisa shared her likes, dislikes, and dreams for what she wanted to do when she graduated. It was this teacher who sparked Lisa's interest in science. The teacher even convinced the school to allow Lisa to take eleventh grade biology in the tenth grade. Lisa loved the material so much that instead of reading adult novels from the library, she began to read anatomy, physiology, zoology, and other science books. Lisa entered the science fair for the first time. School became such a joy in her life that when the bus didn't pick her up one day she hitchhiked to school. She still remembers the lecture she got about hitchhiking, but says "it was worth it."

The teacher also exposed Lisa to "normal" family life. The teacher lived at home with her parents and would invite Lisa to church functions and dinners at her home. The teacher's father, who was a pastor, treated his wife with respect. There wasn't any yelling and they prayed before meals. It was during those dinner conversations about God that Lisa says she began to emerge from her shell. By far, her tenth grade year was her most memorable.

During her tenth grade year, other changes took place as well. Her father leased out his store, which meant that she didn't have to work there during the summer and would have more free time. It also meant, however, that she had to spend more time with her mother. To avoid her mother, she spent time with her friend and tenth grade teacher attending a Christian summer camp. For the first time, she felt "safe and comfortable." At the end of the summer, Lisa's new-found happiness and security came crashing down: she learned that her school was closing its doors, which meant she wouldn't see her favorite teacher and would have to start over at another new school.

Again, Lisa felt like an outsider and alone. For the most part, all of the students in the new school, except Lisa, attended the same church; Lisa's mother had received special permission to let Lisa attend the school. It was far away from home, which meant Lisa had to travel by bus, including a transfer, one hour each way for school. No one befriended Lisa; rather the other students ostracized Lisa because she didn't attend their church, wore pants on the weekends, and listened to praise and worship music. She was so miserable that just one year after becoming interested in science, in eleventh grade she missed more than thirty-one days of school. Instead of going to school, she would stay home and look at pornography, take pills, and cut herself.

Surprisingly, no one knew the turmoil she struggled with. In fact, during eleventh grade, Lisa became a young person's leader in church and worked at the church daycare during the summer. Lisa quickly discovered that she loved working with children:

> "My main desire for working with children at that time was to make sure that I didn't become like my mother. I was determined not to be like my mom and I knew for me that the only way to accomplish that goal was to work with children and work on learning new skills. I had read enough by then to know that if you wanted to change the cycle of abuse, you needed to practice the appropriate skills. I was so scared that I would turn into my mother because of all the literature I had read about the cycle of abuse. I was determined to stop it, even at age 16. I promised myself I would never hurt a child. I promised myself I would never yell at a child. I promised myself I would never belittle a child and that I would always look for something positive. I promised to always praise a child. I really enjoyed sitting and playing with children. I kept my word and soon became known as the 'gifted child who works with children.'"

She fooled so many people into believing that she had it all together that the Pastor sent parents of wayward children to Lisa for counseling. Outwardly, Lisa personified the perfect student, child, and leader. No one knew that Lisa was herself a troubled child, engaging in multiple addictions. She began to read self-help books on how to overcome loneliness and on how to find love. Books again became her only friends. Bored with, and ostracized from, her new school, Lisa began to "stir the pot."

> "I was the one who tried to get away with not wearing hose. I was the one who would get others in trouble by talking about forbidden topics."

To combat the boredom, she convinced her mother to enroll her in a chemistry class at the local community college at night. Despite taking college Chemistry 101 at night, she was still bored. Some of her teachers at the school decided to order a college level correspondence course in Christian Counseling for her. "I loved it and began to research and write lengthy papers. I concentrated on God and faith." In twelfth grade, the high school principal convinced another teacher to supervise Lisa in an independent study course in biology. The teacher rekindled Lisa's interest in science. At home, however, Lisa struggled with loneliness and desires to commit suicide. "I would not give in though because I was not going to let my mom win."

By the time Lisa entered eleventh grade, she had gained the courage to stand up to the abuse she suffered at the hands of her mother. Lisa remembers the day when she defended herself against her mother's attempt to abuse her. After that, the physical abuse stopped. Unfortunately, her mother continued to be verbally abusive to Lisa, telling her that she was evil and no good. She would command Lisa to leave the house, at times backing her into a corner and telling her never to come back. Although her mother would always eventually relent, the damage was done. Years later, Lisa shared that the old saying "sticks and stones will break my bones but words will never hurt me is untrue. For years I was hurt and haunted by the words she said to me."

Finally, graduation day came. She graduated with high honors. However, because she had missed nearly sixty days of school during her last two years the school refused to let her walk down the aisle with honors. Lisa didn't let it get her down, though, because she was already enrolled at a local community college, with the intention to study as a pre-med student. The chapter of her life known as childhood had closed, but was not forgotten.

Nearly twenty five years later, in 2008, Lisa reflected on her childhood and how God had worked in her life to break the cycle of abuse:

> "I think back on these times in my life and am amazed at God's love and how He took care of me. I also reflect and see that I have been stubborn all my life. Stubborn in the fact that I have tried to find my place in this world and stubborn in the fact

that I have gone my own way instead of God's way. Living in survival mode as I so often did kept me from living a life that God wanted me to live. I don't know why He allowed me to be born in a family that abused me. I do know, however, that He provided for me along the way by sending me people that provided a shelter in the storm.

I do not know the exact reason why the Lord allowed me to grow up in the circumstances that I did. However, I do know that all things work together for good for those who love the Lord. (Romans 8:28). Even though I did not grow up in a Christian household or in a loving environment I do not have to allow my past to dictate my present. I do not have to become a secular statistic. God saves and changes lives. I remember being older and sharing with a friend who also had grown up in an abusive environment, similar to mine, that I believed that my past was not a coincidence and that it didn't have to rule my life. She was offended and told me that her past has taken away her joy and that she lost a piece of her innocence. As hard as it may be to read this, I do not agree with what my friend said and you don't have to either. I believe that God can free us, and He has freed me from my past. I do not have to allow it to affect any of my relationships.

For example, statistics say that I am not supposed to be a good mom. Statistics say that because I was abused as a child that I am supposed to abuse my child. I can tell you that I defy statistics. The cycle of abuse has stopped with me. I refuse to allow it to live on. I put it to death by laying it at the cross of Jesus. He takes it and I do not ever have to live it again. People tell me that I am a loving, caring, and sensitive mom. I did not go through any training to be a mom. I did not attend any parenting classes. I did not sit down with a mentor prior to my daughter's birth. So, how did I do it? How did I break from my past? I remembered my Bible verses that I learned when I was in third grade. I remembered how even though I lived the life I did, I am still living on this earth today and have choices to make. I surrounded myself with godly people. I leaned on God's principles. If I did not have that Bible training in third grade and in the Christian schools I attended, I would have struggled more. I may have become a statistic. I cannot explain it any other way.

Today, my daughter is seven and I am diligent to teach her about the traps of Satan. We talk about how God allows Satan to test us so that we can grow closer to God. We talk about our sin as something that separates us from God. We talk about how our actions will win or lose people for the Lord. My daughter and I have been having these talks since she was three years old. It is never too early to talk about the pitfalls of life. A favorite Bible promise of mine is 'Train up a child in the way he should go and when he is old he will not depart from it.' (Proverbs 22:6). For those of you thinking that you can't break free from your past or that you can't be a good parent because you did not grow up in a Christian home, please remember that neither did I. I am grateful, however, that in my growing up years I had a wonderful Sunday school teacher in the third grade who taught me how to memorize scripture and a Christian teacher in the tenth grade who took a personal interest in me. Both of these teachers took the time to expect the best out of me. Both teachers took the time to tell me that God loves me and that they loved me. God knew I was hurting and He provided me with a blessing through these teachers. It did not take a lot of time either on their part. Anyone can help a hurting child who needs just a little time and attention to experience what the Bible tells us about them — that each one is uniquely created, and loved, by God."

Chapter Two

An Unhealthy Childhood Led to Unhealthy Relationship Choices

As I explain in a bit more detail in chapter six, I am not trained as a doctor, psychologist, pastor, or counselor — I am a lawyer. So, what you will read in this chapter is not intended to be medical or professional advice. While I firmly believe that there is no "gay gene" that destines people to be homosexual, with no hope of change, I will not attempt to prove that point here with scientific evidence. I do, however, have a number of great resources for you to consider if you are interested in reading on that topic.[1] Instead, I will offer a layman's understanding, based on reading dozens of books and studies written by the professionals with various perspectives on the issue, attending conferences where some of the leading researchers have spoken on this issue, and speaking with those who have struggled with same-sex attractions. The purpose of this chapter is to help people understand how childhood experiences play an important part of leading some to develop same-sex attractions.

Let us start with the most controversial aspect of the discussion — whether people are born gay. The best way I can explain what I've learned on this subject is to say that some people seem predisposed (emotionally and psychologically) to struggle with same-sex attractions. When you combine the predisposition with certain life experiences, some are more inclined than others to be attracted to those of the same-sex. This is not a foreign concept, but, rather, is common to many kinds of addictions. We just don't usually hear the major media or educational outlets explaining homosexuality this way. Think about alcoholism. We often hear people explain that certain people are predisposed to be alcoholics. We all understand that it wasn't simply the first drink the person took that caused him to become an alcoholic, it had to be combined with certain life circumstances (for example, depressed over the death of a loved one, loss of a job, or end of marriage, etc.) to foster the environment for a problem with alcoholism. If the person who is predisposed to alcoholism took his first drink on the happiest day of his life, when the impact of the alcohol didn't create a euphoric feeling that permitted him to escape from the sad realities of his life, perhaps he wouldn't have craved the additional drinks to help him escape longer and further from reality. The differing results arising from predispositions can also be seen in children. Anyone with more than one child, or who is around children, quickly realizes how siblings are hard-wired differently. A child might have a particular temperament that predisposes him to lie in order to get his way but with the proper training, guidance, and prayer, the child isn't destined to be a criminal — life influences play a big role and ultimately personal choice is the final determining factor. Homosexuality seems to fall into this category. And one of the biggest factors that influences whether a child or adult will pursue same-sex relationships is his upbringing; more specifically, the significance of the relationship between the child and his parents cannot be overstated.

For men with temperaments that predispose them to same-sex attractions, two key life factors are (i) the lack of a strong father-son bond, and (ii) same-sex abuse as a child. For women, two key life factors are (i) the lack of a healthy relationship between mom and dad and (ii) sexual abuse (primarily opposite-sex) as a child. I'll start with the men. Remember, we are speaking in general terms — there are certainly people for whom all the "right" circumstances are present and yet the person never struggles with same-sex attractions. And, certainly, there are those with very unhealthy family dynamics who do not struggle with same-sex attractions. By discussing the generalities, I hope to give you a glimpse of what "causes" same-sex attractions.

Picture for a moment, a boy who is artistic, sensitive, talkative, and, as is frequently the case, not very athletic. Now imagine that his father has made clear that he had dreamed of having a boy that would be a star athlete. At some point, in some way, the father conveys his disappointment to his son, either expressly or implicitly — perhaps the father doesn't spend time with his son or takes no interest in his son's more artistic interests. The son soon realizes that he hasn't lived up to his father's expectations and that he's different (since the kids at school also make fun of his interests and personality). It doesn't take long before the son wishes he could be more like his father. Soon, the desire to be more like his father leads to the son idolizing other boys and men who have all the characteristics he believes that he is lacking. In essence, he idolizes all that he thinks he is not. As he gets older, the feelings change from idolizing to a longing to be close with men — to be attracted to them. From the son's perspective, he hopes that having a sexual relationship with a man he perceives to be all that he is not will fill the void in his life, will make him feel whole, but it does not. In a simplistic way, it's similar to when a girl or guy begins dating someone "out of his or her league." By dating someone "above" himself, the guy believes it elevates his own status.[2]

You can change the fact pattern many ways, including a loving father who works such long hours in an attempt to provide for his family that he doesn't take the time, or even know how, to express signs of affection for his son. Unfortunately, the boy misperceives the lack of attention as feelings that his father does not love him, that he does not measure up to what he should be. If a boy who is dealing with these feelings of inadequacy and self-doubt is sexually abused by an older man, it could send him more quickly down the path of struggling with same-sex attractions — finally, he has a man in his life who cares for and loves him; finally, he feels wanted. To a young boy dealing with self-esteem and identity issues, same-sex sexual abuse only compounds the struggles with same-sex attractions.

Before turning to the discussion of female same-sex attractions, I want to mention briefly the influence of mothers on a son's struggle with same-sex attractions. Years back, I remember hearing for the first time that overly protective mothers who smothered their sons caused homosexuality in their sons. At the time I first heard that, I was a relatively new mother at the time, with an infant son at home, and found myself observing mothers and sons to see whether they fit what I thought was the proper mother-son relationship. I learned a bit later that it's not always that straightforward. While a domineering mother who looks to her son to meet emotional needs unmet by her husband can have negative effects on her son, you can't simply blame it on poor mothering. Regardless of the reasons, unfortunately, under those circumstances, because the mother is the one providing all the attention, it's natural that the son will begin to emulate the mother, adopting her mannerisms and perspectives on life. In the meantime, the boy's unmet needs for love, protection, and guidance from his father continues to grow, taking him further down the cycle mentioned above of idolizing, which turns into emotional and sexual attraction.

For women, a proper relationship with both mother and father play very important parts in the daughter's healthy development. From the mother, the daughter develops her sense of the woman she wants to be; from the father, the daughter learns healthy respect and love of a man. If the daughter sees in her mother everything she doesn't want to become as a female, it opens the door to the daughter's failing to accept a healthy female identity. If the mother is abusive, domineering, unloving, and constantly critical of her daughter, the daughter doesn't bond with the mom and misses out on the opportunity to learn what it means to be a woman. Or perhaps the mother is abused by her husband and the daughter internalizes the abuse in a way that she promises never to be a weak, submissive woman like her mother; again, the daughter doesn't learn what it means to be a woman. In both situations, the daughter lacks a role model of womanhood and motherhood.

From her father, a daughter needs to be shown unconditional, healthy love and acceptance. The father needs to model for the daughter how a man should treat a wife and how a man should respect a woman. If the father is abusive, distant, and unloving, the daughter will seek the love and affirmation in other places — in the arms of someone else who showers her with love and affection. The importance of the father-daughter relationship to the development of a healthy self-esteem in girls is not new. For decades, we have known that if a daughter lacks the proper love and affection from her father, she might look for it in the arms of boys at school, perhaps leading her down a path of early sexual activity. Combine the lack of a proper relationship with her father and the daughter's perception of her mother as weak and submissive at the hands of an abusive father, it creates a female identity that does not appreciate being a woman but at the same time does not like men. It makes a same-sex relationship something worth considering.

Let's further complicate the situation by the fact that girls and women tend to have very close female friends, and that those female relationships are an important part of developing a woman's healthy self esteem and identity. In today's culture, however, girls are told that strong attachment with and feelings toward another female might mean she is sexually attracted to girls; it's a recipe for disaster. In fact, many have written during the past few years about the explosion of young girls experimenting sexually with other girls — it's cool, it's comfortable — it's "bisexual chic."[3] Some of the same thinking made Katie Perry's song, "I Kissed a Girl" so popular.

I realize that this is, for any medical or counseling professionals reading this, a simplistic explanation of a very complicated and controversial topic but, as I stated at the beginning of the chapter, I wanted to introduce those reading this book to what experts have found concerning the "cause" of same-sex attractions. Most importantly, I believe looking at the root of same-sex attractions helps us understand that people can choose to resist and overcome same-sex attractions — just as they can choose to resist and overcome alcoholism, drug abuse, and an array of other negative temperaments and addictions. Not everything that we may be hard-wired to do is necessarily good for us. In fact, as Christians, we know that our natural instinct often is to choose that which is bad for us. If we were to blindly follow where our sin nature led us, we would make all sorts of unhealthy choices and fall into the trap of believing we had no choice to do otherwise.

I also hope that by understanding why a healthy relationship between parents and their children is important, you can get a glimpse into why I believe we must continue our efforts to preserve marriage as the union of one man and one woman. Usually, when I say that in court, there is an attorney from the ACLU, Lambda Legal, NCLR (National Center for Lesbian Rights), or the City of San Francisco telling the judge that what I'm really saying is that women should be at home, in the kitchen, barefoot and pregnant — that I'm trying to impose some sort of discriminatory notion of gender roles on all of America. What these attorneys (and others) fail to understand is that I'm trying to make the obvious point that children need a mom and a dad. Unless the goal is for two women to raise only little girls to marry other little girls, or for two men to raise only little boys who are to then marry other boys, a same-sex couple necessarily deprives the child of (i) either the opposite sex or same-sex role model and (ii) a model of how men and women should treat each other in a marriage. Let's start with the second point first.

Some might suggest that two women or two men in a relationship can model a proper marriage relationship, that the child does not need to have the female-male marriage dynamics modeled. Most people reading this book, however, can probably rattle off a dozen books or articles that highlight the differences between men and women — "Men are from Mars and Women are from Venus" is just one example. If you've been married for any length of time, or in a long term relationship with someone of the opposite sex, think for just a moment about all the things you've discovered that make the point of just how different men and women are. Learning to communicate and work through the differences is something that a husband and wife can model for their children. Since present statistics show that somewhere between 95-99% of children will grow up identifying themselves as having heterosexual attractions, it's vitally important for them to see the husband-wife paradigm modeled.[4] Even more important, however, is the first point mentioned above — role modeling by the opposite or same-sex parent.

Let's start with the need for girls and boys to have a father. As mentioned above, a healthy relationship between a girl and her father is vital for her to develop a healthy self-esteem and to learn to understand how a man should respect and love her. Similarly, the lack of a healthy relationship between a boy and his father is one of the most common factors found in young boys who struggle with same-sex attractions. What happens when a young boy or girl is intentionally deprived of a father by being raised by two women? Not surprisingly, studies are showing that young women raised by two women are more sexually active at an earlier age than their peers.[5] After all, as discussed above, the lack of a healthy relationship between a father and his daughter leads the daughter to seek that affirmation and love in other places. Studies also have long shown that boys without fathers are at substantially higher risks of ending up in our criminal courts and ultimately in a prison.[6] Fathers really do matter.

I realize all of this is a generalization, that there will be exceptions to every general statement, but unless you buy into the idea that maleness and femaleness are wholly irrelevant, you simply cannot say that it makes no difference whatsoever whether a child has a father and mother. The sociological studies reaffirm what we all know instinctively — it does matter. Time and again the studies show that a child does best educationally, psychologically, emotionally, and physically when raised by his mother and father. Naturally, abusive home conditions negatively affect the outcome.

Lisa's life is just one example that bears out what the studies have said for years. She had a domineering, abusive, emotionally detached mother and, for the most part, an absent father because her parents divorced when Lisa was young. Lisa grew up not wanting to be like her mother. Her mother also raised her to distrust men and to have a skewed view of a healthy sexual relationship. In other words, she lacked the necessary love and affection from both her mother and father, was taught to distrust men, and learned to dislike being a woman. To cope with life, she developed several addictions before she even graduated from high school: pills, eating disorders, smoking, pornography, and cutting. Is it really a surprise that after her marriage to a man failed and she hit rock bottom, she was willing to try a same-sex relationship? After all, could things really get worse? She knows now that they could, and did.

Chapter Three

What Led Lisa to Choose the Homosexual Lifestyle

On August 18, 1990, Lisa was married, to a man, amidst plain-clothed police officers inside the church and armed police guards in the parking lot. The police presence was necessary because,

> "A week prior to my wedding, my mom had threatened to kill my fiancé. I didn't take it seriously because I was used to her behaviors, but since she had a loaded gun and would not give it to me when I asked for it, my future mother-in-law called in police reinforcements. In addition to the police, my best friend's parents sat outside my mom's parking lot for surveillance purposes. My brother was unable to attend the wedding because he was inside my mom's condominium making sure she did not leave. The pastor who married us told me later that night before my honeymoon that she had never heard such a sigh of relief after she pronounced someone 'husband and wife.'"

Lisa married at the age of 21, having met her husband two years earlier in a college chemistry class. Lisa says that she was the "trouble maker during labs because I always managed to mess up my experiments." It wasn't that she couldn't do the experiments but she couldn't focus. Again, God sent a teacher to intervene in Lisa's life:

"The chemistry teacher was a little woman of stature with white hair who was never seen without a lab coat. She knew her stuff and expected the best of us. I remember her telling the class that we were in college now and that she expected us to all make A's in her class! One day, after another near explosion in the lab, my teacher pulled me aside and asked if I had eaten anything. I admitted I did not. From then on, she always had an orange for me to eat. That simple act of kindness warmed my heart."

At this time, Lisa was still deep into her food addictions, going days without eating anything but lettuce. Even though home life was less volatile because she had moved from her mother's house to her father's, she still felt the need to be in control of something. "Food addictions give you a sense of having control but, in reality, they control you."

Lisa got involved with her husband because he was persistent. At first, he wanted to be her lab partner, but she refused. Then he kept asking her out to lunch, but she said no. His relentless pursuit became a game to her — another thing to be in control of. Eventually, she agreed to a lunch date. At this same time, another man had been pursuing her, a man who was working on earning a pastoral degree. He was enrolled in the community college because he had little money and wanted to get his basic credits out of the way prior to attending pastoral college. When this man called Lisa at home, she had her family lie and say she was busy. Eventually, unlike the man who became her husband, this man gave up pursuing — he quit "the game."

As she looks back years later, she believes that in choosing the man she did, she turned her back on God. At the time, her dream was to become a doctor so she could do overseas missionary work. She was involved in church and strongly advocated missions. She had already gone on one mission trip and desired to spend her life serving the Lord. Unfortunately, she still struggled with all of her prior addictions, except pornography; after she left her mom's house, she had stayed away from it. The young man whom she eventually married didn't share in Lisa's dreams and desires to do missions work. She wonders what choice she would have made if someone had explained to her what purity and modesty looked like, or what a healthy relationship should look like. Instead, she chose the one who pursued her the most because it was nice to feel wanted. In making her choice, she believes she "let Satan win."

Lisa's relationship with her new boyfriend ushered in many changes. They skipped classes together, spending time talking about women's rights, religion, and politics. He convinced her that creation was faulty and that evolution was true. He told me,

> "I was sheltered and that if I stuck with him he would show me the world! Well, it seemed as if he had opened a completely new world for me. I experienced the world, as I have never done so before — with another person and not by myself. I clung to him. He was the first person who told me I was pretty. He was the first grown up that told me I was intelligent. He was the first person who told me that my parents were wrong in the way they treated me. We engaged in intimacy that only should be between a husband and wife. I allowed him to convince me that it was okay because he loved me; he was the only one who cared about me. I was in too deep to back out. I felt guilty and shameful. I didn't know who to talk to for advice or help because if no one believed me when I was a child who was going to listen to me as an adult? I stopped going to church. Again, I let Satan win in my life."

Eventually, Lisa transferred from community college to a four year college. Her boyfriend, on the other hand, struggled in school. She described him as "very intelligent," but he couldn't stay focused. While they dated, she took care of him. "It was a job that I was very comfortable fulfilling. I took care of my mom. I took care of my boyfriend." He didn't finish his degree and Lisa recalls that he was upset when she was accepted to all the schools to which she'd applied. In August 1998, Lisa began attending James Madison University to finish her pre-med education.

She was both excited and afraid to begin the new adventure. She had never been away from home by herself. Lisa and her boyfriend pledged to date only each other while she was away. Before she left for college, however, he introduced Lisa to what would eventually become her sixth addiction — alcohol. He didn't just introduce her to alcohol, but to hard liquor. Vodka quickly became her drug of choice. "It was easy to get, easy to drink and no one knew what I was doing. I began mixing my pills with the booze and became a totally different person! I drank every weekend. I wasn't the fall down drunk but rather I was the binge drinker. Drinking allowed me to forget my problems and I did not feel guilty until after the drug wore off."

They became engaged when Lisa was twenty, and she married at the age of twenty-one. On her wedding day, her father bet that the marriage wouldn't last more than two years. Lisa says that "I myself had doubts but was too stubborn to turn back. I remember thinking that I should not get married but was not about to allow my dad to win." At this point in her life, she was far from God's best plan for her life. She hadn't been to a Bible preaching church in years and was willing to get married just to prove her father wrong and to avoid hurting the feelings of those who worked so hard to put the wedding together, including her in-laws.

You could say that the relationship was doomed from the outset. Her husband had had a failed relationship and came from a family that struggled with their own interpersonal family issues. By the time she got married, Lisa describes herself as a "classic binge drinker." Rather than taking time to develop a relationship with her new husband, she spent time drinking. She also was completing the last year of her undergraduate degree, working a part time job, and volunteering as an editor of a national child abuse protection newsletter. She says that she felt her husband was more controlling than she would have liked — to the point that she soon felt trapped just as she did as a child.

After she graduated from college, she intended to pursue a master's degree in education but didn't. Instead of going to graduate school, she eventually began working at a psychiatric hospital for children. She soon learned that she could relate to what the children were struggling with in the hospital. At the hospital, "an entire other world opened up to me. I was working with children who were hurting. These children were placed in the locked facility because they were at the end of their ropes. Some of these children had bludgeoned their moms with metal rods, some had hurt animals, while some were so sexually abused they could not function. The average stay at the hospital was approximately 4 months and we had to use restraints and locked seclusion rooms to keep them from hurting themselves, or others. We frequently had to search the children for lighters and sharp instruments."

The stress of the job and a work schedule that conflicted with her husband's did nothing to help build their relationship.

While working at the hospital, Lisa met her "first self-proclaimed lesbian." Their shift, 3:30-11:30 p.m., was a difficult one. Many of the children spent the daytime hours in seclusion or in their rooms because they could not sit through the classes that were taught in the hospital. By evening, they had energy to expend. Each day brought new experiences. After the last child was safely in his bed, she and her co-workers would play cards and talk. On their days off, they would go out drinking. It was during one of the drinking sessions that one of the co-workers confessed to Lisa that she was in a relationship with another woman. Lisa recalls,

"I was floored. But, I also was fascinated. She said she had felt like she had never felt before. She also was abused as a child and didn't have a positive relationship with her mom. I did not know what to think or expect. I was definitely lured by the adventure of the lifestyle, with the prospect of a good relationship with another person. At one point, I told her that I thought perhaps I was a lesbian. She assured me I was."

At about this same time, Lisa decided she needed a less stressful job. She was drinking heavily and taking pills. She also felt depressed about her life. Although hard to imagine how she thought it would be less stressful, Lisa applied for a job as an assistant director of a shelter that worked with adults with mental disability and other secondary illnesses. Shortly after she took the new job, she became very depressed:

> "I could function in the workplace but, at home, my light had gone out. I would sleep, only to be woken by my husband when he returned home from school. I would not eat unless he made me. This went on for four months until he gave me an ultimatum. He told me that I either needed to voluntarily get help, or he'd get help for me. He knew I knew exactly what he meant because just a year earlier my family went through the process of committing my mother to the psychiatric ward against her will. He saw my fear as I came home at 3:00 a.m. that morning telling him how my brother and I had to watch as my mom was thrown to the floor and handcuffed in her own home because she ran from the police. He saw me go through anguish as I went to visit her in her padded cell. He saw me die inside as I testified that she was mentally ill. He knew I knew what it meant to be committed against your will. I was not going to take any chances. I wanted to still be in control. I submitted to his will for the first time in my marriage and sought help."

There's no question that Lisa needed help. Unfortunately, she didn't get the kind of help that she really needed. When she attended the seminar on depression, people told her she didn't "look depressed." When she approached a social worker at the end of the presentation to ask for help, the woman assumed Lisa was a college student attending for extra credit because she didn't seem like she needed help. "Satan was working even then, trying to convince me that I was not sick and I didn't need help." Finally, the social worker agreed to see Lisa. Twenty minutes into the first session,

> "she excused herself and came back with a book for me to read. I was flabbergasted because the book was about women who were abused as a child and who were continuing to be abused

as an adult. It was about the cycle of abuse. I was shocked because I did not divulge the abuse I suffered as a child to her; I was very calculated throughout the intake session as to what I would tell her. She gave me my first assignment of therapy. I was to read at least one chapter of the book each day. I did not only read one chapter, I devoured the book. I had finished the entire book by the next session!"

Lisa's marriage quickly fell to pieces. "Within three weeks, she told me that I should separate from my husband. Although my brother offered to get me a job at the company where he worked, which would have allowed me to live close to his family (and therefore be around people who were attending church), I decided to live with my mother-in-law instead." Although Lisa's husband wanted to try and make the marriage work, in the end, they separated, telling the family it was only temporary, even though they both knew the marriage probably was over.

It was during this time of counseling that the seeds of homosexuality that had been planted while she worked at the hospital began to develop roots in Lisa's life. As she looks back at that period in her life, she can testify to the wisdom of Psalm 1:1. "Blessed is the man who does not walk in the counsel of the wicked." In seeking counseling from a woman who did not love the Lord, she could not help Lisa make choices that were honoring to the Lord. Ultimately, the counseling led her further into a life of rebellion against God, into her seventh addiction — homosexuality.

Chapter Four

The Consequences of Lisa's Choice to Enter the Homosexual Lifestyle

D uring the year that Lisa lived with her mother-in-law, she fell further into her addictions. At the age of 25, she attempted suicide with a deadly combination of alcohol and pills. Looking back,

> "I know that the Lord saved me from a physical death because there was no way that I should have lived. I was in a coma for eight hours, in the intensive care unit for seven days, in the regular medical unit for another two days, and then in the psychological ward for ten days. It was during this hospital stay that I was told by a counselor that I was a homosexual. As part of my treatment, in order to be released, I had to meet with my immediate family, including my husband, and tell them that I was 'a lesbian.' I complied, and, not surprisingly, my marriage ended. Even though I left behind all my childhood addictions at that time, sadly, I entered into the addiction of homosexuality."

With nowhere else to turn, and convinced by others that she must be homosexual, she immersed herself in the "gay culture," surrounding herself with a new "family" of friends. She even became involved in a community organization that advocated for "gay rights." "I engaged in the homosexual life-style for more than seven years. I tried to leave the lifestyle at one point, only to be persuaded by a therapist that I had simply chosen the wrong partner and that I should give it 'one more try.' I stayed in the lesbian lifestyle because I did not know what else or who else to turn to." She was lonely, empty, and confused. Her new friends and lifestyle, however, offered her companion-ship, a sense of purpose, and yet another wrong place in which to search for answers to her hurting heart.

It was at an Alcoholics Anonymous meeting that Lisa met the woman who would eventually be on the other side of the protracted interstate custody battle — Janet Jenkins. The two women met in the late 1990s shortly after Lisa's mom died. The death of Lisa's mother also was a tragic event in Lisa's life: Lisa's mother had been dead in her own home for more than two weeks before Lisa found her. Dealing with the emotions of her mother's death, Lisa turned to others to find comfort. This time, it was with Janet.

When they met at an AA meeting, both women lived in Virginia and soon began an on-again, off-again relationship, with Lisa eventually moving in with Janet. Although Lisa explains that the relationship wasn't a good one, it wasn't any worse than what she had dealt with in the past. Unfortunately, as in the past, pornography played a big part of the relationship between Lisa and Janet, re-introducing that addiction into Lisa's life.

When Vermont became the first state in the Nation to legalize same-sex relationships, Lisa and Janet traveled to Vermont for a short trip in December 2000 to legalize their relationship. Not unlike many women in unhealthy heterosexual relationships who think having a baby will improve their strained marriage, Lisa thought this sign of commitment would improve her relation-ship with Janet. Not surprisingly, it didn't. Soon after their trip to Vermont to enter into a civil union, Lisa, then 32, wanted to be a mom. She says that Janet didn't have any interest in being a mom, but told her that she wouldn't stop Lisa if she wanted to have a baby. At first, Lisa tried to adopt a special needs child in Virginia. When that proved unsuccessful, she sought a solution through assisted reproductive technology: she would be artificially inseminated with sperm from an anonymous donor. With the help of a doctor in Virginia, in 2001, Lisa became pregnant.

The pregnancy was difficult, and doctors told Lisa from the outset that the baby probably wouldn't survive. "At two weeks of pregnancy, the doctor told me that I was going to miscarry because my hormone blood count was dropping. I was supposed to be having multiple births, but by the time of the third blood test, Isabella was the only child remaining. At that point, he put me on anti-miscarriage drugs. Despite the drugs, I remained sick and at six months of pregnancy, I went into labor. The doctor never expected me to deliver a healthy, or even a live, child." At six months, she was put on bed rest and given stronger medications to delay labor. It was during those two months of bed rest that God tugged at her heart:

> "during the two months of bed rest and terrible sickness, I acknowledged God. I remembered how God had helped me through my childhood when my mother allowed me to attend church. Scripture verses began to resurface in my mind. I began to pray, and talk, to God. From the time I had tried to leave the homosexual lifestyle to the time of my pregnancy, God had been convicting me about my living in sin. I would push Him away, though, and continue to live in sin. When I was on bed rest, however, I did not push Him away. I even took my Bible off the shelf and began reading it for the first time in years. Once again, though, instead of putting my complete trust in God, I made a bargain with Him. I promised God that if He would save my baby, then I would leave the homosexual lifestyle. God did save my baby. Isabella was born healthy and strong on April 16, 2002, four weeks early. I did not keep my covenant with God though. Instead of leaving, I moved with my then partner to Vermont, hoping again that things would get better. When the relationship got worse, I became scared for my daughter's future. It was then that God brought to mind the covenant that I had made with Him just months

earlier. I knew enough from my religious background that one does not make covenants with God and not keep them without suffering negative consequences. When my daughter was 17 months old, I left the homosexual lifestyle and moved with my daughter back to my home state of Virginia, where she had been conceived and born."

Lisa vividly remembers how God used a casual acquaintance she met in Vermont to prod Lisa to leave the homosexual lifestyle. In late July or early August 2003, Lisa was trying to become a representative for a company that sold wellness products so she could save enough money to be able to leave Janet. A woman who was already a sales representative for the company took Lisa out to dinner. Although they didn't really know each other, she looked right at Lisa during dinner and said "What are you going to do when Jesus tells you that what you are doing is wrong?" She then apologized, telling Lisa she had never confronted anyone like that before. Lisa, however, saw it as a sign from God. "I told her that it must be of God because I was trying to leave Janet. Three weeks later, this woman helped me pack my things so I could move."

God also used Lisa's brother to help her leave the homosexual lifestyle. He and his wife helped her move to Virginia by giving her money for housing and moving expenses. She even began attending her brother's church. It was at that church in Virginia that God continued to work in Lisa's life. In September 2003, Lisa asked God for forgiveness of her sins and, for the first time, understood what it meant to have a personal relationship with Jesus Christ. "It was that night that I became a new creature in Christ. No longer was I bound to the sin of homosexuality." As you'll see later, though she was no longer a slave to her homosexual attractions, it was an ongoing struggle to overcome the addictions and emotional scars.

Wanting to officially end her former relationship, and in obedience to what she says the Lord directed her to do, in December 2003, without the help of an attorney, Lisa sent papers by mail to the family court in Vermont to dissolve her same-sex civil union with Janet. Because Virginia did not, and still does not, recognize same-sex relationships, Lisa could only officially end the relationship in the place where she had entered into it — Vermont. Lisa did not expect what happened next. "To my dismay (but God already knew what would happen), I was challenged for custody of my daughter."

Shockingly, Janet claimed to be Isabella's second mother, even though she admitted, as she must, that she is not biologically related to Isabella. Nor did Janet adopt Isabella under Vermont's second parent adoption law. Instead, Janet claimed she was a mother because she wanted to be a mother to Lisa's child and had been involved in the lives of Lisa and Isabella until Isabella was 17 months old. Lisa quickly realized that she needed to find an attorney to represent her in Vermont. She let her first attorney go after a few months when the case wasn't progressing quickly enough. Looking through the yellow pages and searching the internet, she found a firm that dealt with same-sex civil unions. During the intake process, she was directed to the firm's expert in civil union law, Deborah Lashman. Unbeknownst to Lisa at the time, Ms. Lashman played a prominent role in the legal history in Vermont in the area of same-sex parentage. In a landmark 1993 case from the Vermont Supreme Court, Ms. Lashman and her same-sex partner changed the law concerning adoption. The court ruled for the first time that a same-sex partner could adopt her partner's biological children. Lisa knew nothing about the case (since she wasn't from Vermont and wasn't involved in the homosexual lifestyle in the early 1990s) because the case only bears the initials of the two children who were the subject of the litigation — BLVB and ELVB. Ms. Lashman didn't bother to tell Lisa about her case either.

Thirty minutes before the first hearing on the case, in March 2004, Lisa finally met Ms. Lashman. As the court transcripts reveal, and a story in The Washington Post Magazine recounts, Ms. Lashman told Lisa the case needed to proceed as a regular custody case (just like one between a husband and wife concerning their biological children), with Janet being treated as a parent to Isabella. She told Lisa that she believed Vermont law required the court to treat Janet as a parent. When Lisa told her in the hallway that she objected to that strategy, Ms. Lashman refused to go along with Lisa's request that they oppose the idea of treating Janet as a parent. Months later, Ms. Lashman

admitted in court that she had no Vermont case law to back up her position and never told Lisa that there was a way under Vermont law for Lisa to
challenge Janet's argument that she was a parent. Instead, during the hearing
in March 2004, Ms. Lashman told the court that Lisa waived her right to
raise any argument that Janet was not a parent. After the hearing, when Lisa
demanded that Ms. Lashman take steps to reverse what she had done in court,
Ms. Lashman refused and terminated the attorney-client relationship with
Lisa. In other words, without Lisa's consent or knowledge, Ms. Lashman told
the court Lisa waived any rights she had to challenge Janet's claim that she was
Isabella's second mom.

When Lisa's next attorney, Judy Barone, came back to court in May, she
pleaded with the court to revisit the parentage issue — to undo the waiver
made by Ms. Lashman. She begged the court to apply existing Vermont law
to rebut Janet's parentage claim. Under Vermont law, there is no law that
specifically treats a same-sex partner as a parent to her partner's child or that
explains who is a parent when a child is born to any couple (opposite or same-
sex) by assisted reproductive technology. Instead, the law generally states that
partners in a civil union should be treated the same as married partners in a
heterosexual relationship. Under Vermont law, there is a presumption that the
husband is the father of any children born to the wife during the marriage.
If parentage becomes an issue (as it sometimes does in a custody or child
support case), a husband or wife has the right to challenge that presumption
by showing, through genetic tests, that the husband has no biological connec-
tion to the child. Lisa's new attorney argued that Lisa should have had the
same right to show, through genetic tests, that Janet is not a parent to Isabella.
The court refused to revisit the parentage issue, instead issuing an order in
June 2004 that granted Janet liberal, unsupervised visitation in both Virginia
and Vermont with then two year old Isabella.

Realizing that Vermont had no intention of respecting her rights as
Isabella's biological mom, Lisa filed papers in Virginia, asking Virginia
to declare her Isabella's only mother pursuant to Virginia law. The law in
Virginia, where Lisa and Janet met, and where Isabella was born, states that

a child only has one mother. In October 2004, the Virginia court did what one would expect under Virginia law — the trial court declared Lisa to be Isabella's only mother. With that decision, the parties began five years of legal volleying between the Virginia and Vermont courts. In November 2004, Vermont officially declared Isabella to have two mothers — Janet and Lisa. To its credit, the court at least admitted what it was doing — creating new law in order to reach its decision. The judge explained:

> "Parties to a civil union who use artificial insemination to conceive a child can be treated no differently than a husband and wife who, unable to conceive a child biologically, choose to conceive a child by inseminating the wife with the sperm of an anonymous donor. The issue of parental status of a child conceived through artificial insemination [either for civil union or married couples] is one of first impression in Vermont.... The court adopts the reasoning of [two] other courts that have determined that where a legally connected couple utilizes artificial insemination to have a family, parental rights and obligations are determined by facts showing intent to bring a child into the world and raise the child as one's own as part of a family unit, not by biology."

Stated differently, the court admitted that the Legislature still hadn't answered the question of how a child born by artificial insemination by an anonymous sperm donor would gain the legal status of a child to the spouse who was not biologically related to the child. After deliberation, the legislature could decide that the husband automatically becomes a parent once he signs the consent form for the doctor performing the procedure. Or, the legislature could decide that the husband would need to adopt the child after birth. What was clear is that the state did not have any law in the area so the court created one. Not only did the court create new law in Vermont, but it then applied it to determine parentage of Isabella even though she was born two years earlier, *in Virginia*. Based on that decision, Janet then asked Virginia to honor the Vermont visitation order.

Before relating what happened next in the litigation, it is important to clarify some facts about the Vermont court case. There are at least three pieces of misinformation that have been regularly repeated over the years, as if they somehow change the fact that Lisa is Isabella's only biological parent. These are: (i) Lisa stated in the papers she filed in December 2003 in Vermont that Janet was a parent to Isabella, (ii) Lisa asked in the papers she filed in Vermont that Janet be given parentage rights over Isabella, and (iii) because Lisa filed in Vermont to dissolve her civil union, she somehow waived protection under Virginia's laws that declare same-sex relationships void and unenforceable.

First, Lisa never stated that Janet was a parent to Isabella. What some have pointed to is Lisa's honest answer to a question on the standardized form Vermont uses to dissolve a civil union. That form asked Lisa to list "the biological or adoptive child of said civil union." Because Isabella was Lisa's biological child, born during the civil union, she listed Isabella in that box.

Based on a checked box on the standardized form, it's also been argued that Lisa asked the court to treat Janet as a parent to Isabella. Lisa called the court, asking for help on how to fill out the form concerning the custody matters. The clerk she spoke with told her she had to fill out all the boxes concerning child custody and support since a child was listed on the form. She proceeded to check the first box, which asks that Lisa be awarded legal rights and responsibilities (legal custody) for Isabella. She then checked the next box that asked that Lisa be awarded physical rights and responsibilities (physical custody) for Isabella. It is the next box that has garnered so much attention. The next box asked her to check whether plaintiff (Lisa) or defendant (Janet) should be awarded suitable parent child contact (visitation). Since Lisa asked for legal and physical custody to be awarded to her, she had to check defendant in this box. Even though she checked the box, she hand wrote on the side that any parent-child contact awarded to Janet should be "supervised." Nothing on these forms reflects Lisa's intentions to give up her rights as Isabella's sole biological parent so that Vermont could treat Janet as a second mom to Isabella.

At the time Lisa left Janet, it is true that Lisa was willing to let Janet see Isabella in Virginia if Janet requested a visit. Those visits, however, would be arranged through Lisa and subject to her supervision. Over time, after Janet sought full custody of Isabella for herself with only visitation for Lisa, after Lisa grew in her understanding of her Biblical obligation to raise her child according to the truth of Scripture, and in order to protect Isabella from the destructive lifestyle choices of those involved in homosexuality, she no longer thought it was in Isabella's best interest to have any contact with Janet. As Isabella's biological mom, that choice was Lisa's, not the court's, to make.

Finally, there are those that suggest Lisa somehow lost any protection she had under Virginia law because she lived in Vermont for a year after Isabella was born and because she filed court papers in Vermont. There is no question that had Lisa not filed in Vermont, and Janet also had not filed in Vermont within six months of Lisa having left Vermont, this case probably would have turned out very differently. Those facts, however, do not obliterate the marriage laws passed in Virginia. The reality is that Vermont should not have allowed Lisa and Janet to enter into a civil union in Vermont in the first place. In Virginia, where Lisa and Janet lived, same-sex relationships were not legal or recognized. Under Vermont law, if a heterosexual couple had tried to go to Vermont to enter into a marriage forbidden by their home state (because of age requirements, too closely related, etc.), a Vermont statute expressly required courts to treat the attempted marriage illegal. In other words, Vermont doesn't permit opposite sex couples to get married in Vermont to evade the laws of their home state. Vermont, however, refused to apply that same law to civil union couples even though Vermont's civil union law required same-sex couples to be treated the same as married couples. When Lisa argued that Vermont should never have let Lisa and Janet, who were Virginia residents, enter into a civil union in violation of Virginia law, the Vermont Supreme Court refused to apply the statute to same-sex couples. Thus, under Vermont law, same-sex couples are entitled to come to Vermont to flout the laws of their home state while opposite sex couples cannot do the same. In other words, same-sex couples are given special treatment.

Most importantly, what Lisa did in entering the civil union in Vermont and then filing papers in Vermont to end the relationship does not change

Virginia's laws. One person cannot undo laws passed by the legislature and an amendment passed by the people: Virginia law says all same-sex relationships are void and unenforceable in Virginia. The laws provide for no exceptions. Regardless of what Lisa did, the Vermont relationship and resulting custody order should not have been recognized in any way in Virginia. Nevertheless, in August 2005, a Virginia court said Virginia would honor the Vermont custody order. This result was shocking when you consider how broad Virginia's laws are. The statute prohibiting recognition of civil unions states:

> "A civil union, partnership contract or other arrangement between persons of the same sex purporting to bestow the privileges or obligations of marriage is prohibited. Any such civil union, partnership contract or other arrangement entered into by persons of the same sex in another state or jurisdiction shall be void in all respects in Virginia and any contractual rights created thereby shall be void and unenforceable."

The Constitutional amendment similarly states:

> "This Commonwealth … shall not create or recognize a legal status for relationships of unmarried individuals that intends to approximate the design, qualities, significance, or effects of marriage. Nor shall this Commonwealth or its political subdivisions create or recognize another union, partnership, or other legal status to which is assigned the rights, benefits, obligations, qualities, or effects of marriage."

Faced with such clear, broad language, many have wondered why Virginia courts decided to let Vermont's decision to redefine family and marriage control what happens in Virginia. The answer is simple — an improper understanding and interpretation of the obligation that one state has to give full faith and credit to another state's orders. Contrary to common understanding, the obligation in the United States Constitution to give full faith and credit to another state's orders does not require a state to ignore its public policy decisions on who is a parent and what is a family. I'll explain why in more detail in the next chapter.

For the next four years, numerous appeals were filed in Vermont, Virginia, and before the United States Supreme Court. Time and again, Vermont ordered visitation to take place and Virginia courts said Virginia had to honor the visitation orders. Although Lisa did comply with a few court orders requiring that she give visits to Janet, including a one week unsupervised visit in Vermont, she stated in court papers that she refused to give further visits when she saw the psychological trauma the visits put Isabella through. After the visits, she and others testified that Isabella was a different person — clinging to her mother, withdrawn from others, and acting out. Isabella's behavior concerned one teacher so much that she reported it to social services.

When Lisa refused to give further visits, Janet asked for Vermont to award her full custody of Isabella, with visitation to Lisa. She also repeatedly asked that Lisa be monetarily sanctioned and jailed for refusing to give visitation to her. At one point, Janet's attorneys even tried to use Lisa's religious beliefs as a basis to switch custody. They argued that Lisa could not make proper decisions for Isabella because Lisa believed that "God has a plan and purpose for Isabella's life," "in God's order, marriage means the union of one man and one woman, a child cannot have two mothers," and "God gave Isabella to me by forming her in my womb."

Through it all, God was working in Lisa's life:

> "I have grown closer to Him through my trials. I have come to Him with a broken and contrite spirit and He has given me rest and peace. I know that He will not give me any more than I can handle. God has turned my stubborn spirit and the grief of my past into a joy of my salvation. It has been a joy to walk with Him. My trials have given me opportunities to share Christ. I believe that my past can be used to help others and that God can use my past-repented sin for His glory and honor. He is doing that now through my interstate custody battle and I praise him and give him thanks for all things."

As anyone who knows Lisa will attest, throughout the course of the litigation she truly did have a peace from God that surpassed all understanding.

After each court battle, she would send me encouraging e-mails because she thought I needed them. In two e-mails she sent during summer 2009, she shared incredible wisdom with me. In the first e-mail, she talked about a sermon she had just listened to entitled "God enjoys the impossible." The pastor talked about how God often lets the problem get really big so that when He ushers in victory, He is glorified. She told me,

> "Rena, He will be glorified. He is waiting for that seemingly impossible moment — which could be now or could be later — to show Himself strong. I plan on continuing moving forward, living my life as I have, standing for Him. I can go to man or I can go to God. I am going to give God an opportunity to show himself strong. I pray that I don't take it out of God's hands. I plan on allowing Him perfect control over the circumstances."

That e-mail echoed something she wrote three years earlier, "Faith involves risk, a challenge beyond the normal." And she reminded me in the second e-mail what she was fighting for:

> "I am standing for God's laws — that marriage is between one man and one woman. I am also standing for Virginia's marriage laws that state the same fact as God's laws. This battle is not only about Isabella and me, it is about parents' rights everywhere in the nation. Isabella is a political hostage and is being used by the gay agenda to push their agenda of gay marriage. They say and have said in the past in regard to gay marriage that it will not hurt anyone. Well, they are wrong — a little seven year old girl is being hurt and they want to rip her away from her biological mom (me) and give her to a legal stranger. We are still a Christian nation and I believe it is a Christian's duty to stand for what is right in God's eyes. I still put my trust in God and am blessed that He has been

and still is with me every step of the way during this almost six year litigation. Please continue to pray that God protects and provides for Isabella and me and that He will turn the heart of the judges toward the truth, which would be to rule according to Virginia's laws."

Chapter Five

Understanding the Interstate Custody Battle

Those who have followed Lisa's case frequently ask "why does Virginia have to recognize the Vermont custody order when Virginia passed one of the strongest laws in the country refusing to recognize orders arising out of same-sex relationships?" The short answer is that it does not. Courts, however, have improperly applied to custody battles arising from same-sex relationships a 1980 federal law passed to address a then-growing problem of biological parents fleeing with their children to another state in search of a better custody order. Congress never intended for that law to apply to a child born to a same-sex partnership where only one of the partners is a biological parent to the child. More importantly, even if Congress had intended for the 1980 law to apply to same-sex relationships, as I will explain below, the U.S. Constitution does not give Congress the authority to require states to uniformly enforce orders from other states that re-define marriage and family.

Article 4, section 1 of the United States Constitution states that "Full faith and credit shall be given in each state to the public acts, records, and judicial proceedings of every other state." Congress has authority to decide "the manner in which such acts, records, and proceedings shall be proved, and the effect thereof." All that means is that Congress is authorized to pass a law explaining what documentation is required to move a valid order from one state to another state and what effect the order will have in the new state.

Litigation in cases like Lisa's revolve around the question of what the Constitution means when it grants Congress the authority to decide what "effect" an order has in a new state.

Although I'm not one who believes that the U.S. Constitution means whatever the U.S. Supreme Court says it means (because the Court's rulings are just the opinion of nine, or, more often, five, people, which may or may not be a correct interpretation of the U.S. Constitution), the logical starting point is to explain how the Supreme Court has interpreted this constitutional provision. The United States Supreme Court has explained that the "effect" clause of Article 4, section 1 means that an order from one state's court "gains nationwide force" for purposes of "claim and issue preclusion (res judicata)." This means that the court order will be recognized nationwide as having determined the contested legal issue between the parties that was the subject of the court order. Stated differently, if Jim sues John over a contract dispute and wins $5,000, Jim can't go to another state to re-litigate the same question of whether Jim is entitled to $5,000 under the contract. However, that does not answer the question of how the second state must react to the order — most importantly, does it have to enforce the order and, if so, how will it enforce the order. The Supreme Court has explained it this way: to say that an order gains nationwide force for purposes of claim and issue preclusion "does not mean that States must adopt the practices of other States regarding the time, manner, and mechanisms for enforcing judgments. Enforcement measures do not travel with the sister state judgment as preclusive effects do; such measures remain subject to the even-handed control of forum law."[7]

In other words, based on the Supreme Court's interpretation of the Full Faith and Credit Clause, while Virginia might have to recognize that litigation took place in Vermont so that Virginia courts are prevented from re-litigating custody or parentage concerning Isabella, Virginia remains free to choose whether and how to enforce the Vermont order under Virginia law. Essentially, the full faith and credit clause stops Virginia from re-litigating the custody issue to reach a different result, but once the Vermont order crosses the border into Virginia then Virginia's laws, not Vermont's, determine if and how the order will be enforced.[8] Let's take a look at a couple of examples.

A common set of facts where this occurs concerns title to land. If an Arizona court, either as part of a divorce decree between Sally and Joe, or probate of John's will where Joe and Sam are heirs of John, decides that title to land located in Texas belongs to Joe, the state where the land is located (Texas) is not required to enforce the Arizona order and transfer title of the land to Joe (i.e. enforce) if Texas' laws or public policy prohibit it. Because of claim or issue preclusion, however, Texas could not re-litigate the question of who has title to the land but it can't be forced to change the name on its record books concerning land ownership because Arizona said it should.

To use a more contemporary example, a resident of one state (where there is no, or a very low, homestead exemption to protect homeowners from a creditor's forced sale of their home) obtains a judgment in California for $300,000 against a resident of Florida (which has an unlimited homestead exception protecting the home from forced sale by creditors) and seeks to enforce it in Florida. While Florida would be required to give full faith and credit to the $300,000 judgment in terms of recognizing that John has a judgment against Joe (and therefore that Joe can't re-litigate the issue again in Florida), Florida would not be required to enforce the $300,000 judgment according to California law. Instead, Florida would follow its own laws concerning time, manner, and mechanisms for enforcement of money judgments, which in this case would mean it couldn't be enforced against the homeowner. Even if the Florida debtor (Joe) had no job, no income, and no other property except for his home with equity of $1,000,000, the creditor could not enforce his $300,000 judgment by way of a forced creditor sale in Florida because Florida exempts the entire value of the home from such a sale. Some may remember that OJ Simpson's home in Florida was protected against his creditors for this same reason.

The Supreme Court has applied the same enforcement distinction with respect to rights that a second state must give to a child adopted in another state. For example, in 1915 the United States Supreme Court decided a case that answered the question of whether an adoption in Louisiana required Alabama to treat the adopted children as heirs for purposes of inheriting land owned by their adopted father in Alabama. At the time, for purposes of inheriting land, Alabama law excluded from the list of "descendants" those who had been adopted. The Supreme Court explained that while the full faith and credit clause prevented Alabama from re-litigating the issue of whether the children had been properly adopted in Louisiana, it did not require that Alabama afford the adopted children rights contrary to the laws of Alabama.[9]

In Lisa's case, Virginia is entitled to follow its own laws concerning the time, manner, and mechanisms for enforcement. Virginia is entitled to look to Virginia law to determine how to enforce the out of state order. With respect to orders arising out of same-sex relationships, Virginia law is clear: such orders are not enforced at any time, in any manner, or by any mechanism. Virginia law does not carve out any exceptions — any and all rights, benefits, and obligations flowing from same-sex marriage or a same-sex civil union are "void in all respects." Virginia has no mechanism in place to enforce a custody determination that is based on Vermont's decision to declare Janet a parent because of her same-sex relationship with Lisa.

Those who argue that Virginia must give full faith and credit to, and enforce, the Vermont order rely upon the 1980 law mentioned earlier — the Parental Kidnapping Prevention Act ("PKPA"), 28 U.S.C. § 1738A. The PKPA was passed to address a rising number of cases where a mother or a father in the midst of a custody battle would flee to another state with the children to re-start the custody litigation in the hopes of getting a better decision. Because child custody orders are by their nature always subject to change (modification) until the child becomes an adult, courts in some states refused to give full faith and credit to child custody orders from other states. Those states would declare that because the orders were not "final orders" (as compared with final money judgment obtained at the end of a contract dispute), the second state was free to decide whether to give full faith and credit to the other state's orders.[10]

At most, the PKPA elevated child custody orders to the same status as "final orders" for full faith and credit purposes. It also attempted to "'avoid jurisdictional competition and conflict between state courts,'" by preventing one parent from ignoring the court order and re-starting litigation in a second state.[11] As a result, a second state is deprived of jurisdiction (authority) to enter a custody order once another state has properly exercised its jurisdiction to issue a custody or visitation order.[12] The PKPA, however, does not require a second state to *enforce* the first state's order or to treat child custody orders differently than other final orders for purposes of enforcement. In other words, child custody orders are subject to the same time, manner, and mechanisms exception to enforcement that all other orders are subject to.

This is further demonstrated by the specific placement of the PKPA in the United States Code. In 1790, Congress adopted the Full Faith and Credit Act pursuant to the authority granted to it in Article 4, section I, to state what effect orders have in a second state. That law was codified as title 28 of the United States Code (U.S.C.) § 1738. The PKPA was codified in the same place — 28 U.S.C. § 1738A. The United States Supreme Court has explained that the placement of the PKPA as an addendum to the Full Faith and Credit Act is itself "strong proof" that Congress intended child custody orders to have the *same* operative effect as do other acts, records, and judicial proceedings that fall within the mandate of the Full Faith and Credit Act.[13] Therefore, the PKPA is subject to existing full faith and credit exceptions, including the enforcement exception mentioned earlier. The Supreme Court stated,

> "The PKPA, 28 U.S.C. § 1738A, is an addendum to the full faith and credit statute, 28 U.S.C. § 1738. This fact alone is strong proof that the Act is intended to have the same operative effect as the full faith and credit statute.... [I]t seems highly unlikely Congress would follow the pattern of the Full Faith and Credit Clause and section 1738 by structuring 1738A as a command to state courts to give full faith and credit to the child custody decrees of other states, and yet, without

comment, depart from the enforcement practice followed under the Clause and section 1738."[14]

As discussed earlier, that enforcement practice is one where the receiving state enforces the other state's order according to the laws of the receiving state, not the ordering state. In fact, Congress does not have constitutional authority to mandate enforcement. Because the Constitution requires states to give full faith and credit (which the Supreme Court has expressly stated means res judicata effect/claim preclusion, not enforcement), and the Constitution grants Congress authority to provide the manner in which foreign orders shall be proved for purposes of that full faith and credit obligation (which authority it invoked in passing the PKPA), Congress lacks constitutional authority to mandate *enforcement* of foreign orders. Congress only has constitutional authority to direct res judicata effect (i.e., can't re-litigate the issue), not enforcement. Thus, the answer to the question of whether Virginia must enforce the Vermont order is an easy one — no, because Congress lacks authority to require Virginia to enforce the order. In the years of litigation, no one has yet offered a response, because none exists, to the fact that the Constitution limits Congress' authority to require states to enforce all orders from other states. To the extent that courts interpret the PKPA to mandate interstate enforcement, they are wrong.

Let's assume just for a moment that Congress had authority to mandate enforcement. In analyzing the interplay between the PKPA, the federal Defense of Marriage Act ("DOMA"), and Virginia's marriage laws, the relevant issue becomes whether anything in the PKPA shields the PKPA from application of then-existing or later-enacted exceptions to the full faith and credit requirement. A brief review will help explain the question. Before Congress passed the PKPA, child custody orders were not covered by the full faith and credit obligation and thus a state could decide whether it wanted to recognize the foreign order. After the PKPA, child custody orders were elevated to the same level as final orders. So, if there were exceptions (such as the time, manner, and mechanism exception) that applied to the full faith and credit obligation concerning final orders, they would now apply to the PKPA as well. If Congress had intended to single the PKPA out for unique full faith and credit treatment, exempting it from application of pre-existing or later-enacted exceptions to the full faith and credit obligation, or from the full line of cases explaining the full faith and credit obligation, it would have needed to expressly state that intent. Nothing in the PKPA's text or legislative history, however, reflects any such intent.

The full faith and credit obligation created in the PKPA for child custody orders is therefore subject to several exceptions: a longstanding public policy exception for matters of state rather than federal concern, the enforcement exception discussed above, and the exception expressly codified by Congress in the federal Defense of Marriage Act ("DOMA").[15] Consistent with both the longstanding public policy exception concerning state law matters and the enforcement exception, DOMA provides that each state can determine for itself what legal effect to give to: (a) same-sex marriages; (b) same-sex relationships treated as marriage, but not called marriage; and (c) rights or legal claims arising from same-sex marriages or same-sex relationships treated as marriage.[16]

A House Judiciary Committee Report issued just prior to the vote by the House on DOMA explains that:

> "While the Committee does not believe that the Full Faith and Credit Clause, properly interpreted and applied, would require sister States to give legal effect to same-sex marriages celebrated in other States, there is sufficient uncertainty that we believe congressional action is appropriate.... The Committee therefore believes that this situation presents an appropriate occasion for invoking our congressional authority under the second sentence of the Full Faith and Credit Clause to enact legislation prescribing what (if any) effect shall be given by the States to the public acts, records, or proceedings of other States relating to homosexual marriage." [17]

Some have said that DOMA only gives a state the authority to refuse to recognize a same-sex marriage but has no effect on child custody orders arising out of those same-sex relationships. That same Congressional report further clarified, however, that it was concerned about much more than whether a marriage license or civil union certificate would be valid in a second state:

> "In the abstract, it is difficult to know precisely what conse-
> quences would result if a same-sex couple from, say, Ohio, flew
> to Hawaii, got 'married,' returned to Ohio, and demanded that
> the State or one of its agencies give effect to their Hawaiian
> 'marriage' license.... In general, the Committee believes that at
> least two things would occur.... First, the State law regarding
> marriage would be thrown into disarray, thereby frustrating
> the legislative choices made by that State that support limiting
> the institution of marriage to male-female unions.... Second,
> in a more pragmatic sense, homosexual couples would
> presumably become eligible to receive a range of governmental
> marital benefits. For example, ...child custody and support
> payments; spousal support; premarital agreements; name
> changes; nonsupport actions; post-divorce rights; evidentiary
> privileges; and others."[18]

This language highlights that those who passed DOMA were concerned that each state should be able to decide for itself whether to recognize a same-sex relationship and whether to make statutes dealing with child custody, premarital agreements, and spousal support applicable to same-sex relationships.

It is important to point out that DOMA did not create a new full faith and credit exception but instead recognized at the federal level that "domestic relations are preeminently matters of state law."[19] Although not many people talk about the federalism aspect of the U.S. Constitution, the fact is that the Constitution is one of limited, enumerated powers. That means that the federal government lacks power to do anything unless the Constitution expressly gives the federal government the authority; all powers not expressly granted to the federal government are retained by the states. As James Madison explained during the ratification process of the U.S. Constitution, the powers retained by the states under our Constitution "are numerous and indefinite .... The powers reserved to the several states ... extend to all the objects which, in the ordinary course of affairs, concern the lives, liberties, and properties of the people, and the internal order, improvement, and prosperity of the state."[20] In contrast, "[t]he powers delegated ... to the federal government are few and defined.... [The federal powers] will be exercised principally on external objects, as war, peace, negotiation, and foreign commerce...."[21] Therefore, it is no surprise that the United States Supreme Court has explained that "[t]he whole subject of the domestic relations of husband and wife, parent and child, belongs to the laws of the states and not to the laws of the United States."[22] DOMA confirms this understanding — leaving to each state the ability to decide whether to give effect to same-sex relationships and any orders arising out of those relationships.

Because Congress did not exempt child custody orders from then existing or future exceptions to the full faith and credit obligation, child custody orders are necessarily subject to the exception expressly codified in DOMA for all orders arising out of a same-sex relationship treated as marriage. Virginia exercised its sovereign power to enact one of the strongest prohibitions in the Nation against recognition of same-sex unions and orders arising from them. The language is clear and comprehensive in its treatment of rights arising out of same-sex civil unions: any and all rights, benefits, and obligations flowing from a same-sex civil union are "void" and "unenforceable" in Virginia.[23]

In Lisa's case, the Vermont order also cannot be enforced because the orders giving Janet custodial and visitation rights all arise from Vermont's unconstitutional decision declaring Janet to be a parent to Lisa's child. Virginia can not be required to enforce an unconstitutional order. The decision to declare Janet a parent is unconstitutional for two reasons: the Vermont order (i) unconstitutionally infringes Lisa's parental rights and (ii) violates federal due process guarantees.

First, let's look at the parental rights argument. The United States Supreme Court has explained that the right of a biological parent — Lisa in this case — to direct the upbringing of her child is a fundamental right.[24]

This shouldn't surprise us given that the Bible makes clear that parents (not government) are responsible for educating their children.[25] More specifically, parents are instructed to raise their children in the fear and admonition of the Lord.[26] A parent's fundamental right has been described as "perhaps the oldest of the fundamental liberty interests."[27] The Supreme Court has explained that because "[t]he child is not the mere creature of the State,"[28] "[i]t is cardinal … that the custody, care and nurture of the child reside first in the parents, whose primary function and freedom include preparation for obligations the state can neither supply nor hinder."[29] Sadly, over the decades, we have watched the Supreme Court diminish the importance of that unalienable right. In the Court's latest statement on parental rights, some of the Justices significantly limited the scope of the right.

In 2000, the Court analyzed a Washington statute that permitted any third party (non parent) to seek visitation with a child. Under that statute, once the third party filed a petition for visitation with the court, the court would decide whether visitation with the third party was in the child's best interest. In other words, at *any* time, *any* third party could ask the court for a visitation order and a judge would decide whether visitation was in the child's best interest, regardless of whether parents objected to visitation. The Supreme Court declared that the application of the law in that case unconstitutionally infringed the parent's rights, stating that in deciding a third party claim for visitation, the constitution at the minimum requires that at least "some special weight" be given to the parent's preference.[30] Thus, when a third party seeks visitation, letting the court decide whether it is in the child's best interest to have visitation with the third party unconstitutionally infringes upon the parent's fundamental rights. According to the Supreme Court, the court is to presume that fit parents act in the best interests of their child and then give their preference *some* special weight. Although the "some special weight" standard could offer slightly more protection to parents than the Washington statute, it still significantly interferes with parental rights because it allows the government to override a parent's decision based on "some special weight" rather than that the parent is unfit or somehow causing actual harm to the child.

No matter what giving parental preference "some special weight" means in the face of a third party request for visitation (because no one seems to understand what exactly that means), the Vermont courts failed to meet that standard. The Vermont orders treating Janet as a parent to Lisa's child failed to give *any* special weight whatsoever to Lisa's preference as the sole, biological parent. In fact, no constitutional analysis whatsoever was performed prior to declaring Janet, a legal stranger to the child, to be a parent. Instead, the court declared Janet a parent (because she was in a same-sex relationship with Lisa at the time Isabella was born) and then stated that as a parent she had the same fundamental rights as Lisa.

It's important to keep in mind that Janet was not given visitation as a third party (as a grandparent might be) but was given full rights as a parent.[31] As a result, she and Lisa stood on equal footing before the court as it decided who should be given custody and who should be given visitation. Because the orders fail to afford Lisa the constitutionally guaranteed minimum of "some special weight," they are plainly unconstitutional under existing Supreme Court precedent and Virginia should not have enforced them.

The Vermont orders also should not have been enforced because they are based on a retroactive application of a new parentage rule created by the Vermont courts during the course of Lisa's case. Retroactive application usually refers to the situation where the legislature passes a law and applies the law to circumstances that arose *before* passage of the statute. For example, when Congress passes a law making something a crime for the first time, that law can not be applied to conduct that took place before the law was passed. Because it violates procedural due process guarantees to punish someone after the fact for conduct that was not prohibited at the time the conduct was engaged in, the U.S. Constitution and many state constitutions prohibit retroactive application of laws. The Supreme Court has explained that the due process and ex post facto clauses "safeguard ... interests in fundamental fairness (through notice and fair warning) and the prevention of the arbitrary and vindictive use of the laws."[32]

Although the Supreme Court has limited the federal Constitution's ex post facto clause to criminal laws, both Vermont and Virginia prohibit stripping people of substantive legal rights retroactively (after the fact) in civil proceedings as well.[33] Because Vermont law did not give Janet parental rights at the time Isabella was born, or when the lawsuit was filed, the legislature could not have passed an act that would have retroactively stripped Lisa of her parental rights by giving parental rights to Janet. The rationale underlying the prohibition of retroactive laws made by the legislature, i.e., that a person cannot be stripped of substantive rights without notice or fair warning, should apply equally to judicial rulings (particularly since judges lack authority to make law).[34] Therefore, the Vermont orders, based upon a new parentage rule applied retroactively to deprive Lisa of her parental rights, are unconstitutional. The full faith and credit obligation, which requires interstate recognition of valid judgments under most circumstances, shouldn't have been used to compel Virginia to enforce an unconstitutional order.

Interpreting the PKPA to require that Virginia enforce an order declaring a third party a parent over the objections of the fit, biological parent, presents yet another constitutional problem in that it would require Virginia (and states with similar laws) to unconstitutionally treat some same-sex couples differently than other same-sex couples. In 2008, in another case, the Virginia Court of Appeals refused to permit a former same-sex partner to obtain visitation rights with the biological mother's child.[35] Christine Stadter and Jennifer Siperko were in a same-sex relationship from May 1999 until the early summer of 2004. On January 2003, Jennifer gave birth to a child. Christine could not adopt the child in Virginia. The child was about 1 ½ years old when the relationship between Christine and Jennifer ended, the same age Isabella was when Lisa's relationship with Janet ended. In September 2004, Christine filed a petition for visitation in Virginia and Jennifer objected. Christine asked the court to grant visitation based on her "asserted status as the child's de facto parent." The Court of Appeals affirmed the lower court's refusal to grant visitation. Relying upon Virginia Supreme Court precedent that interpreted parental rights under the federal constitution, the court explained that, to safeguard a parent's rights, "courts may grant visitation to a nonparent in contravention of a fit parent's expressed wishes only when justified by a compelling state interest." The court further explained that,

> "compelling state interests in the child's health or welfare will operate to overcome the presumption in favor of a fit biological parent in certain specific circumstances, including where a parent 'voluntarily relinquishes' custody and care of a child to a nonparent, or where it has been 'established by clear and convincing evidence that there are 'special facts and circumstances ... constituting an extraordinary reason for taking a child from its parent or parents.'"[36]

The trial court found that there were no such special facts and circumstances and refused to grant Christine visitation and the court of appeals affirmed.

The decision by Virginia to enforce the Vermont orders in Lisa's case directly conflicts with the decision in Christine's case. In Lisa's case, the Vermont courts declared Janet a parent without any showing of special facts and circumstances or any consideration whatsoever of the biological parent's wishes. Nevertheless, the courts in Virginia have directed that an obviously constitutionally flawed order that contradicts Virginia law be registered and enforced in Virginia. Thus, in Virginia, two biological moms, who lived less than three hours apart when the decisions were issued, were treated differently without any legitimate justification. Both women were in a same-sex relationship for five to seven years, both moms ended their relationship when the child was approximately eighteen months old, and both were Virginia residents at the time the relationship began and at the time the child was born. Nevertheless, in one case, the mom's former partner is not afforded parental rights because the Virginia courts have held that granting such rights would infringe the biological mom's constitutional rights; while in the other case, a mom's former partner is entitled to parental rights pursuant to a foreign order that now must be enforced as a valid Virginia order. Under these circumstances, the PKPA, as it is being applied by Virginia courts, violates the federal guarantee of equal protection under the law.

The debate over legal recognition of same-sex relationships has been raging for years, and will likely continue to do so for years to come. After the Massachusetts Supreme Judicial Court redefined marriage to include same-sex couples,[37] an explosion of litigation began that directly challenged marriage laws across the country as unconstitutional.[38] A separate strategy that garnered little national attention, but which proved more successful, involved indirect assaults on the states' marriage laws. Those cases sought court orders to permit same-sex couples to adopt,[39] or declare legal strangers parents of their former partners' biological children.[40] Armed with an order conferring parental rights, one or both of the parties then sought to export those orders to states that expressly prohibited recognition or enforcement of same-sex relationships. This is illustrated in Lisa's case as Vermont's decision to fundamentally redefine marriage and parentage was exported to Virginia and enforcement sought through the full faith and credit obligation despite Virginia's express statutory and constitutional prohibitions against recognition or enforcement of orders arising from same-sex relationships. Unless the PKPA, DOMA, and Full Faith and Credit Act are interpreted properly, core domestic relations matters will, in essence, be federalized.

Not only is this sort of federalization of domestic relations laws inconsistent with Article IV, section 1 of the United States Constitution, but it also poses an immediate threat to the very concept of liberty upon which this Nation is founded. The founders of this Nation knew the dangers of concentrating too much power in the centralized government and purposefully created a federal government of limited, enumerated powers. This separation of the two spheres is one of the Constitution's structural protections of liberty. "Just as the separation and independence of the coordinate branches of the Federal Government serve to prevent the accumulation of excessive power in any one branch, a healthy balance of power between the States and the Federal Government will reduce the risk of tyranny and abuse from either front." In

"America, the power surrendered by the people is first divided between two distinct governments, and then the portion allotted to each subdivided among distinct and separate departments. Hence a double security arises to the rights of the people. The different governments will control each other, at the same time that each will be controlled by itself."[41]

A proper understanding of federalism requires us to remember that as a Nation made up of fifty individual states there are constitutional limitations on the scope of the federal government's powers:

> "The powers delegated by the proposed Constitution to the federal government are few and defined. Those which are to remain in the State governments are numerous and indefinite.... The powers reserved to the several States will extend to all the objects which, in the ordinary course of affairs, concern the lives, liberties, and properties of the people, and the internal order, improvement, and prosperity of the State."[42]

Because the "whole subject of the domestic relations of husband and wife, parent and child, belongs to the laws of the states and not to the laws of the United States,"[43] the federal government has no authority, through an unconstitutional application of the full faith and credit obligation, to reduce fifty domestic relations policies enacted by the people of the individual states to a singular policy developed by a handful of states that choose to experiment with the father-mother family paradigm. Unfortunately, the first state in the Nation to address the full faith and credit issue is improperly ceding its state control over domestic relations matters to Vermont and the federal government.

Chapter Six

Helping Others Make the Choice to Leave the Homosexual Lifestyle

As I sit to write this and the next chapter, I feel the need to be very candid about why you should even consider listening to anything I have to say about the topic of helping yourself or others make the choice to leave the homosexual lifestyle. I am not a doctor of any type, a psychologist, or a personal counselor. I also never lived a homosexual lifestyle. I am, however, someone who has had a great deal of exposure to those (i) in the homosexual lifestyle, (ii) who've chosen to leave the homosexual lifestyle, (iii) who engage in scientific studies concerning homosexuality, and (iv) who counsel those struggling with same-sex attractions. I am also someone whose heart is burdened for those who have made the choice to live a homosexual lifestyle, often not fully appreciating the way in which society has deceived them to believe that this is the best plan for their life. Through the process of writing this book, I am also someone who has discovered how I failed as a personal friend to Lisa Miller — as a Christian friend, I could and should have done so much more to help her through her personal struggles. I would like to make sure that as Christians, we get a glimpse of what we need to do to show Christ's love to those struggling with same-sex attractions. In this chapter, I hope to share my heart both with church leaders and lay people about what I believe they can and should do to better reflect Christ to those struggling with same-sex attractions.

Over the years, as I have been involved with court cases and legislative efforts to protect marriage as between one man and one woman, I have had a number of people tell me that Christians have no right to prevent two men or two women who love each other from marrying each other when the divorce rate among men and women in and out of the Church is so high. While I absolutely agree that there is a huge divorce problem that needs to be fixed, I don't believe that the way to accomplish it is to let same-sex couples marry. Attorney William Duncan analogizes this argument to a Jenga© game. As the Jenga© tower gets taller, and therefore more unstable, everyone watching and playing knows that each block pulled out could be the one that causes the entire structure to collapse. Marriage, as a core, stabilizing institution in society, has been significantly weakened over the years. In large part, the heaviest blows to marriage have come as a result of society's emphasis on temporal happiness and satisfaction over commitment and a Biblical concept of selfless love. We need, as a Church and a society, to take steps to shore up the foundation of marriage, not strike another blow that could cause its collapse.

As Christians, we know that God designed marriage to be between one man and one woman for the purpose of bringing together men and women to create our future generations. It is through the family unit that values are transmitted to the next generation. As Christians, we are to adopt God's view of commitment and love, not society's. Author Maggie Gallagher explains that "[t]o restore marriage we need a commitment both more grand and more gripping, more sacrificial and oh so much more satisfying...."[44] On the other hand, as much as I truly believe that God created, and intended for, marriage to be the union of one man and one woman for life, I do not believe, as some apparently do, that living a homosexual lifestyle is some sort of unforgiveable sin. Let me be clear, though, that I do believe that sexual sins have particularly grievous emotional, psychological, and health consequences for those who engage in them. In I Corinthians 6:18, Paul warns us to flee from sexual immorality, pointing out the unique nature of sexual sin — that all other sins are committed outside the body. While I don't necessarily understand all of the implications of that verse, it is undeniable that sexual sins, whether opposite-sex or same-sex, have a different effect on us than do others and that the memories and images of them can stay with us for a lifetime.

An illustration of the fact that homosexuality is not an unforgivable sin is found at Proverbs 6:16-19. It lists six things the Lord hates, seven that are detestable to Him and neither homosexuality nor any other sexual sin is specifically listed here. Rather, they include the following: haughty eyes, a lying tongue, hands that shed innocent blood, a heart that devises wicked schemes, feet that are quick to rush into evil, a false witness who pours out lies, and a man who stirs up dissension among his brothers. Of course, it almost goes without saying that a heart that devises wicked schemes and one who has haughty eyes include those struggling with sexual sins. In Leviticus 20:11, God speaks of homosexual conduct as detestable, or an abomination, but Paul explains in Romans 1:24-32 that God is displeased with any sexual immorality, including homosexuality. Therefore, homosexuality cannot be set apart as deserving of categorization as the worst or an unforgiveable sin. In fact, in I Corinthians 6:9-11, after Paul lists a variety of wicked sins, including sexual immorality, adultery, and homosexuality, in verse 11 Paul states that "that is what some of you were but you were washed, you were sanctified, you were justified in the name of the Lord Jesus Christ and by the Spirit of our God." That passage offers a clear message of hope and redemption for anyone struggling with sexual sin, including homosexual conduct.

One thing that I believe the Church often misunderstands is that you needn't have struggled with same-sex attractions in order to minister to those struggling with same-sex attractions. Essentially, if you are someone who has ever struggled with issues of insecurity, loneliness, emptiness, poor self-image, or abuse, you can relate to someone struggling with same-sex attractions. Homosexuality is just one way some people seek to meet a legitimate need in illegitimate ways. Maybe you don't turn to same-sex attractions in times of loneliness, insecurity, heartache, or depression but there have been times you sought to fill that void in the wrong way — to what did you turn? Perhaps more to the point, how did you seek to fill that void before you came to know Christ as your savior? If you remember that longing, those desires, the emptiness, then you can relate to someone struggling with same-sex attractions. God slowly revealed that truth to me during the course of the past seventeen years.

It is definitely my sincere desire that by sharing both Lisa's experiences and what I have learned that you will realize now (not after a nearly two decade journey) how to love and minister to those in the homosexual lifestyle.

I grew up in a small town, on a farm, in Michigan. Mine was the typical all-American hometown where we spent weeks decorating floats for the homecoming football game, ate ice cream floats at the local soda shop, purchased candy at the five and dime store, and lined main street with candles for a Christmas walk. I graduated from high school in 1987 and from Michigan State University in 1992, which is a public university then with more than 40,000 students. Through all those years, I had not met anyone who identified as homosexual. It wasn't until I went to law school in New York City that I met students involved in homosexuality. God used the countless hours working alongside students struggling with same-sex sexual attractions to show me that those involved in homosexuality are real people, with real life struggles, who have made choices in their life that led them to involvement in homosexuality. There is one student in particular whom God used in my life. During our hours together, as friends and colleagues, she shared her dreams, life goals, and feelings with me. Nearly seventeen years later, I still vividly recall one conversation in particular that I had with her that made me realize I held some incorrect notions about those involved in a homosexual lifestyle.

We were talking one day and she mentioned that she had met a woman she liked. When she told me that the two of them had "spent the night together," I immediately assumed she had engaged in a sexual relationship with her. When I shared my assumption with her, she kindly but quickly corrected me. You see, I saw same-sex relationships as just about sex and therefore expected my friend to have had a sexual relationship with the woman she had just met. I got a glimpse then of what I later gained a much greater appreciation for — those in same-sex relationships seek what we all seek — to truly be loved, appreciated, and accepted by another, to feel whole and fulfilled. Unfortunately, they've been misled to believe that they can find that satisfaction in a sexual relationship with someone of the same-sex.

Fast forward nine years to the United States Supreme Court case of *Lawrence v. Texas*. In January 2003, I left work as a commercial litigator in New York City to begin working for Liberty Counsel, a non-profit organization, which seeks to restore the culture by advancing religious freedom, the sanctity of human life, and traditional family. Little did I know when I took the job with Liberty Counsel how drastically my life would change. In fact, only a year and a half after I began working for Liberty Counsel, I took the call from Lisa Miller. The first assignment I was given when I began working for Liberty Counsel in January 2003 was to write an amicus brief to the United States Supreme Court in support of Texas' authority to criminalize same-sex sodomy. For those unfamiliar with what an amicus brief is, it is a brief written by those not representing the main parties in the case to offer additional, helpful information to the court. In a case before the United States Supreme Court, dozens of amicus briefs are written in support of each side of the case. In *Lawrence*, Liberty Counsel submitted an amicus brief that contained a section explaining the health risks associated with homosexual conduct. In conducting the research, I was exposed for the first time to the negative health consequences of living a homosexual lifestyle. I read studies and articles, including many from the U.S. Centers for Disease Control and Prevention and leading homosexual publications, that revealed the increased rates of sexually transmitted diseases, cancer, depression, alcoholism, and suicide among homosexuals. In several instances, sexually transmitted diseases are at epidemic levels among homosexuals.[45]

In another part of the amicus brief, we wrote about the meaning of the term "sexual orientation." Although I had heard that there was no "gay gene," this was the first time I researched the issue. For the first time, I realized the complete lack of any scientific evidence supporting the idea that people are born gay. Even more, I was surprised to learn just how much research there was showing the effectiveness of therapy for those desiring to resist same-sex attractions. Even more compelling than the medical studies showing the possibility for change were the stories of those I personally met who had left the homosexual lifestyle behind.

My heart began to break for those struggling with same-sex attractions, who were being deceived by a morally relativistic society that espouses the notion that all lifestyle choices are good and healthy. I also became very concerned over the misinformation schools were teaching our children about same-sex attractions. As I'll discuss in chapter eight, schools were encouraging our children to explore same-sex relationships, at a young age, and telling them that "being gay" is a healthy and normal choice. I was shocked at the lengths to which schools would go to tell our children lies that could harm them physically and emotionally.

A number of issues concerning same-sex relationships took front stage nationally in February 2004 when San Francisco Mayor Gavin Newsom, in consultation with leading homosexual activists, told his staff to violate California law and begin marrying same-sex couples. It was during my time involved in the litigation to defend California's marriage laws that I spent hours, days, and weeks thinking about how to get the court to understand what marriage is and why the state had legitimate reasons to continue to define marriage as the union of one man and one woman.

As I look back now, I know God was preparing me for Lisa's case. When Lisa called Liberty Counsel in June 2004, explaining that a Vermont court had just declared her former same-sex partner to be a parent to Lisa's then two year old child and directed Lisa to give visitation to Janet, we had been prepared to understand that we had to take her case. Not only was the future of a young girl at stake, but the case was significant legally as it was the first of its kind in the Nation. Since you already know the details of Lisa's legal case, let me fast forward to summer 2009 when Lisa shared some of her journals with me. As I read the pages of the journal, I wept because I realized that despite all that God had shown me about same-sex attractions and the homosexual lifestyle, I did not truly appreciate the nature of her struggle to choose to resist same-sex attractions and to attempt to live a lifestyle pleasing and acceptable to God.

I had failed to appreciate the need for those seeking to resist same-sex attractions — to resist a lifestyle they know to be sinful and unhealthy — of friends of the same-sex who loved, accepted, and appreciated them. One thing

I've heard time and again from those previously involved in the homosexual lifestyle is that gays and lesbians know how to "do family," that gay and lesbian friends are there for others who identify as homosexual. As someone who has never been involved in the homosexual lifestyle, I best understand it as analogizing it to a fraternity, sorority, or any other type of organization that links people together based on common interests, values, or characteristics. When you are part of these organizations or societies, you know that the people involved share some common interests and goals, want to be associated with you and enjoy doing things together. Understanding it this way, I believe the homosexual community offers that kind of family experience to those who feel cast aside by society based on their same-sex sexual identity.

Here's an e-mail Lisa received in September 2008 from another woman who left the homosexual lifestyle:

> "Do you ever notice that powerful Christians are really busy and often unavailable? … Too busy raising the perfect Christian family and saving the world from evil to really engage on an ongoing basis? This is going to sound weird, but it almost seems like the gay community does 'family' better than the Christian community. I felt so much more a part of something when I was gay.… We knew each other, understood each other, and embraced each other wholeheartedly. Maybe I am glamorizing it and we simply bonded in our dysfunctional enabling, I don't know."

Lisa shared with me: "She is right about the fact that in some ways the gay community does family better than the Christian family." I believe this is one of those areas the Church can and must improve — we need to be willing to open our hearts and lives to those struggling with same-sex attractions to demonstrate to them, through our lives, the love of Christ. We need to show them that God has something better and genuine planned for them. We also need to "be real" with them, letting them see our struggles with sin.

In that same e-mail, Lisa also explained how the homosexual lifestyle is glamorized. At first, I didn't understand how a lifestyle that leads to so much personal, physical, emotional, and psychological harm could be glamorous. But then I thought about raising children. As any parent (or any adult looking back on her childhood) will tell you, there is a period in the life of most children where the best way to get a child to do something seems to be to convince him that you want him to do exactly the opposite. If you try the direct approach — don't look at the pictures in that book, don't drink what's in this bottle on the shelf, or don't smoke — many children feel compelled at some point to do exactly what you've told them not to; there is something exciting, adventurous, dangerous, and alluring about doing what others say is wrong to do. I believe there is a component of that involved in the homosexual community. Lisa explained it this way: "the homosexual lifestyle is glamorous because it is the new and the 'in thing' to do — it puts you in the spotlight. Coming out [gay or lesbian] is like the socialite coming out parties a generation ago." As Christians, we need to understand that it is very important that we present a real alternative to what the homosexual community is offering — we need to be family for them and we need to show them the true joy of living a life the way their Creator designed them. The importance of being a family to those struggling to leave the homosexual lifestyle cannot be overstated. It's also something all of us are capable of doing — no special training required.

Lisa explained that whenever she fell back into any of her addictions, or even struggled with thoughts about them, it was because "I didn't have my eyes on God but also because I didn't have a support system." In June 2005, she wrote "I have no friends, I don't have anything but work, church, and being a mom. I feel so incomplete." I can't help but wonder how many single moms who have moved to a new area can relate to those feelings of loneliness or purposelessness? Whereas some single moms might turn to other sins to try and fill the void — perhaps getting into an unhealthy relationship with a man, or drinking — Lisa's temptations were those of her past — same-sex attractions and pornography.

What really hit home to me was how Lisa's struggles with same-sex attractions were no different than the struggles with loneliness and insecurity that many of us struggle with. However, when she struggled with those feelings, it would lead her to have inappropriate thoughts of relationships rather than what some of us might turn to. The point was that when she was lonely, with no real Christian family to support her, to love her unconditionally, she desired to fill that emptiness with someone who could make her feel special, loved, and wanted. Whether it was a man or a woman wasn't the point — it was wanting someone to fill that emptiness and meet that need for personal touch and companionship. In November 2005, she hit the nail on the head: "I am angry about my struggles, my life — about being alone — I want to love and be loved." Fast forward to late 2007 and early 2008, when more of her thoughts were about men rather than women, but still she realized that the persistent desires to be married were rooted in her strong desire to be loved. Just as many Christians pursue relationships they know are not good for them because of their desire to be married, to be loved, so too was Lisa struggling with that. For her, because of her past same-sex relationships, she not only had to resist the temptation to pursue unhealthy relationships with men, but also with women. In July 2006, she actually explained that "feelings of same-sex attractions have popped up again but I can just as easily transfer those feelings to a man — it's as if I just want someone to love me." Lisa knew, however, that in God's plan for her, someday she would marry a man God had prepared for her.

As I read through some of Lisa's journals, which she specifically chose for me to read to help write this book, I wept. I easily fell into the description of the busy Christian who didn't have time to truly be there for Lisa. I also know now why she made it a point to share at times with me how she truly appreciated the fact that I didn't judge her — that she felt comfortable exposing her weaknesses to me because she knew I wouldn't judge her. Even still, it wasn't until I read her journals that I truly understood the nature and extent of her struggles. I wish I had known more about her struggles earlier, when perhaps I could have come alongside her. Knowing now what I do about her struggles, I still don't judge her. By not judging, however, I don't mean we give people a pass to continually sin. As Christians, we have an obligation to hold brothers and sisters in Christ accountable. What I mean, however, is that when people are struggling with temptations and sins and truly repent for their mistakes, we don't toss them aside — we don't act as though we don't also have temptations, sins, and weaknesses in our own lives or that their sins are somehow worse than ours. Rather, we should come alongside them as a support system, as an accountability partner, and as someone who shows them Christ's unconditional love as they walk their life in Christ.

Part of coming alongside someone struggling with loneliness and emptiness is helping them realize that God is the only one who truly can fill the emptiness and loneliness in our lives. I like the way Lisa explained it: "Instead of curling up under a blanket when we are down, we should curl up with His love and reassurance — He delivers us because we take refuge in Him." She specifically points out that "God can fill the loneliness when it comes."

Lisa's journals make very clear how loneliness and emptiness can be direct paths to a life back into the homosexual lifestyle. If you think about it, it makes complete sense. For those who came to know Christ as their savior later in life, you might still remember the emptiness and loneliness you felt as a non-Christian; you yearned for something to fill the void in your life, often attempting to fill the emptiness in the wrong ways: drugs, alcohol, gambling, sex, etc. For some people, one of those "wrong ways" is through same-sex relationships. Lisa described it this way in April 2004:

> "Today, I know why I chose lesbianism. Even while I was engaging in the woman to woman relationships, I didn't feel connected to the other person. I felt as if I was caring for them and would become upset when they didn't perform according to how I felt they should. I always felt as if a piece of the puzzle was missing — I filled that void at first by pills, withholding food, cutting, alcohol, pornography, and female relationships."

Lisa's journals offer so many great nuggets for those struggling with same-sex attractions (or any other addiction for that matter). First, she has several words of caution for those tempted by the mindset that "I can just dabble in my addiction without getting trapped." She reminded herself in a December 2006 entry that "small compromises lead to big disasters. To me, a thought is a small compromise that indulges my fleshly appetite." A few days later, she wrote that she was feeling sick, and was tired. She hadn't spent time reading God's word and as a result, "my mind is blank and is quickly filled with wrong thoughts — I revert to my comfort zone of fleshly desires. I need to keep my eyes on God, my focus on his teachings, and my mind crammed full of His word. My heart needs to be filled with His love."

In an e-mail to me, Lisa offered some sound advice about being able to overcome addictions:

> "Remember that your addiction comes in just like a lion seeking its prey — you don't know it until the lion is upon you! Try wrestling a lion off you. No matter what you do, you get scratched. I like to think though that Jesus is the balm that heals the wound. If you don't fight the lion, or someone doesn't come alongside you to help you fight it, then it devours you. That is why confessing our sins is so important. And having Christian influence in your life is vital.... I think the key to overcoming addictions is knowing God and knowing how God made us."

In May 2004, she explained why daily Bible study was so important to her overcoming her addictions. "In the Bible, I learn (1) God's purpose for me, (2) God's truth, (3) I am loved by God, and (4) God's sovereignty." She looked at the Bible as a firewall to keep out unwanted thoughts and feelings.

She also made quite clear that for her the struggle to overcome addictions was a daily one. "I can tell you that the addictions do not just go away. However, God is always there if I call on Him." God used one particularly difficult day in 2009 to remind her that He is there, every day, in the smallest detail:

> "I was trying to get my mind off my problems by serving others but it was not working because there was no one to serve ...

everyone cancelled their appointments that day.... So I put my head down to pray. When my parent helper came back, she handed me an envelope. I asked her 'where did you get this?' She said, 'in your box.' I opened it and it was from an anonymous person who said she heard about my story through the grapevine and that she was praying for me. She also typed out a Bible verse and taped it to the inside of the card. The Bible verse was in red — 'My grace is sufficient for you in your weakness' and a quote below it 'God has tailor made grace for everything we face.' Later that night, a lady handed me a 10 page handwritten letter full of scripture.... She told me in the letter, 'I realize you are and have been attacked on all sides. You are strong, without a doubt. But who are you to attempt to fight this spiritual battle in human flesh? God is in control — trust Him — even when things look the worst, God is in control.'"

After Lisa shared this story with me, she told me that "I think God is telling me I need to let go and let God. I think He wants me to totally trust in Him."

As we spoke, she often wondered if her struggles with same-sex attractions and pornography were the thorn in her side that would continue through the remainder of her life. I recently heard a great sermon discussing II Corinthians 12:7-10. In that passage, Paul discussed the thorn in his flesh that consistently troubled him:

"To keep me from becoming conceited because of these surpassingly great revelations, there was given me a thorn in my flesh, a messenger of Satan, to torment me. Three times I pleaded with the Lord to take it away from me. But he said to me, 'My grace is sufficient for you, for my power is made perfect in weakness.' Therefore I will boast all the more gladly about my weaknesses, so that Christ's power may rest on me. That is why, for Christ's sake, I delight in weaknesses, in insults, in hardships, in persecutions, in difficulties. For when I am weak, then I am strong."

In the sermon I heard, the pastor explained that the reference to a thorn doesn't refer to a little splinter we might get by rubbing against some rough, unfinished wood. Rather, it's more like a sharp, wooden instrument that could be used to impale him. That thorn was used by Satan to continually torment Paul, to beat him down. There is much speculation about what exactly the temptation or torment was — a disease, sinful thoughts, or other ailment. Paul explains that he pleaded with God three times to remove the thorn in his flesh. Yet, God did not remove it. Paul realized that through this unanswered prayer, he became more aware of his need to be dependent on God — he needed to rely on God's strength and grace day by day, moment by moment. The thorn in Paul's flesh kept him humble and dependent on God.

It's interesting when you think about it, but as soon as suffering enters our life, our immediate response is often to ask God to get us out from under the suffering. This passage in II Corinthians reminds us that we need to remember that through suffering, God is able to show us that His grace is sufficient. The pastor giving the sermon gave a definition of grace that really exemplified this: "God doing for me, in me, and through me what I cannot do myself through the person and power of Jesus Christ."[46] God's grace is tailor made for everything we face.

I believe Lisa is one of those rare people who understand exactly what Paul was writing about. She understands that perhaps she will always have the struggles as a way to ensure that she depends entirely on God's grace on a moment by moment basis. She knows the power of prayer and understands that through prayer and fasting she gains a better understanding of her Savior, which allows her to let go of the reigns of control over her life and to let God guide her every step.

Through Lisa's e-mails and journal entries I came to realize that regardless of the sin issue — the individual temptation — there are root causes that many of us share in common: loneliness, emptiness, anger, and feelings of insecurity. Lisa shared about a conversation she had with a pastor, who had told her that in all his years of counseling, he'd never dealt with someone who struggled with addictions to cutting or same-sex attractions. She wrote to me:

"I find that interesting because don't we all have some sort of addiction. Why would we treat a person who has a cutting addiction any different than one who has an addiction to lust or pornography? Biblically, it is our small compromises that lead to great disasters.... I wonder how many other pastors think that drug and alcohol addictions need to be treated differently than homosexuality? An addiction is anything that breaks fellowship with God and anything that we should not be doing (against God's laws) that we can not seem to stop.... Addictions, regardless of the type, can be changed into successes by surrendering those thoughts to God.... I wish I could tell people not to quit before God can do a miracle in their life."

Unknowingly, I too had fallen into the mindset that there was something different about helping people struggling with same-sex attractions and that I needed to leave that to the "professionals" or to others who had struggled with same-sex attractions. I hope that by sharing from Lisa's experience you will understand, as I do now, that regardless of our sin issue, we all have much more in common than perhaps we had thought in the past. And regardless of the sin issue, God's grace truly is sufficient to transform lives.

I can't end this chapter without stressing how important it is to teach our young people to minister to and love those struggling with same-sex attractions. Unfortunately, I've seen an insensitivity among Christians to the "gay" issue, often referring pejoratively to those struggling with same-sex attractions. On the one hand, I am encouraged to see Christian youth realizing that living a homosexual lifestyle is sinful (although many of them should spend a bit more time comprehending that pre-marital opposite sex sexual activity is also sinful). On the other hand, I am discouraged by many Christians' insensitivity to the fact that those struggling with same-sex attractions need Christ. Just as we should not mock or laugh about someone struggling with alcoholism or drug addictions, we shouldn't laugh about, perhaps with disgust, those living a homosexual lifestyle.

Nor should we condone slang phrases, such as "that's so gay," which can be harmful in at least two ways. First, if you use such phrases around a person who is struggling with same-sex attractions (and remember that you may not know the person has those struggles), you add to the existing self-esteem and self-worth issues by reinforcing the inner struggle taking place. Would you call the child who is struggling academically "stupid," or the child who is athletically challenged "clutz?" Then why would we derisively call a man "gay" who perhaps displays effeminate characteristics (and possibly is struggling inside with his sexual identity). Second, think about the impact "that's so gay" has on the person who hears it used by others to describe an undesirable set of characteristics. If a person struggling with same-sex attractions sees you and other Christians throwing the phrase around to refer to what you perceive as an undesirable set of characteristics, would that person feel comfortable opening up to you? Do you think that you have any credible Christian witness left to show him the love of Christ — to show him what it means to have a heavenly father who loves and accepts him? As Christians, we need to ask ourselves whether what we say and do is a hindrance to God possibly using us to witness to a hurting individual. Unless we intend to exclude those struggling with same-sex attractions from our personal ministry, even though the Bible commands us to share the gospel with everyone, we need to deliberately change our hearts and attitudes about those involved in the homosexual lifestyle.

As Lisa and I discussed this book, she wanted to be sure to specifically mention what we, as Christians, should *not* do in our efforts to encourage someone to leave the homosexual lifestyle — do not completely isolate yourself from them, telling them that when they are ready to leave the homosexual lifestyle then you will be ready to help them. Separatism, as Lisa refers to it, can actually cause some people to stay in the lifestyle longer than they otherwise might. Think about it this way: if the homosexual community is very good about being a "family" to those living a homosexual lifestyle, then by separating ourselves as Christians from those we know who are struggling with same-sex attractions, we actually leave them with no other support system but the homosexual community. I understand the good intentions that prompt us to give an ultimatum to people — e.g., if you do this, I won't be there for you. However, if someone we love makes the choice to engage in wrong conduct, we need to maintain an active lifeline of communication and compassion that our loved one can grab onto when she finally realizes her mistake. Remember, however, showing compassion and love does not mean giving the false impression to the person that God condones homosexual behavior: we need to tell them the truth about homosexuality (that it is a sin and harmful in many ways) but with love and compassion. We need to remember that they are lost and hurting, just as each of us once were, and in need of a Savior.

Chapter Seven

Overcoming Her Addictions

Not only has Lisa's legal battle been a long and difficult road, but the struggle to overcome her past addictions and emotional scars was not easy either. As the title of this chapter states, Lisa's journey to overcome her addictions has been a continuing process. For any of us with sin issues in our life (which includes all of us), there are some struggles that we truly do overcome and there are others that seem as though they will be lifelong struggles. A big step in beginning the process of healing and change is to discover the root of the problem, sometimes tracing issues back to childhood.

Lisa refers to her childhood memories as a box crammed full of "pick me ballots" — the type of ballots that get stuffed into a raffle box. Sometimes the ballots are folded neatly, ready to unfold and read. Sometimes the box is so full that some ballots get crammed into the uttermost corners of the box; they make room for other ballots to enter the box but are themselves ready to be forgotten. Still other ballots are nearly worn out, almost illegible, because the person who stuffed it into the box kept folding it smaller and smaller, almost to the point of invisibility. Finally, other ballots get put into the box quickly and unfolded so that they stick to other ballots. These are the ballots that can easily be overlooked, unless a diligent person comes along to make sure all the ballots are considered.

Each of these ballots represents a type of memory. The really good memories in our life are like the ballots that are neatly folded, eagerly awaiting another opportunity to remind us of what's inside. The ones stuffed into the corners are like are the memories of the everyday events in our life — nothing particularly good or bad, but they are there if you dig around and try to remember them. The ballots that are folded over and over again, almost in an effort to be hidden, are the tragic memories in our life, the ones that are almost too horrible to remember, so we try to forget. And finally, there are those ballots that get slid into the box quickly and hide behind other memories. These can represent good or bad events in life but for some reason we hide them away quickly. It sometimes takes diligence and persistence to recall these memories. Regardless of the type of memory, or "pick me ballot," a particular life event represents, it is important to unpack the box in order to understand life choices that were made and to begin the process of healing.

For those who are struggling with same-sex attractions, I hope you realize that you are not alone in your struggles and that there are people who want to help you see the life God has planned for you. To this day, I remember the friends who helped me when I was struggling in life, when I hated God and had a skewed vision of what He was like; they were willing to show me the truth about God and to come alongside me as I desired something more for my life but didn't then know what it was. I knew there had to be something more, something better and eventually I was willing to listen to what they had to tell me about the God of the Bible.

Although I wish Lisa were here to write this chapter, she made very clear as we were outlining this book some things she wanted to share. She wants you to know that she absolutely understands some of the feelings you might be going through. Even though she was not happy in her same-sex relationship, it was comfortable, known, and offered earthly security (money, job, friends, home). When Lisa finally made the decision to leave the homosexual lifestyle, she left behind a job, friends, the security of a relationship, and a home. For her, the choice was staying in a lifestyle she knew was not healthy for her daughter and herself or trusting that God had something better planned for her. Without question, it was a huge step of faith.

Since that time, she's met many women, also with children, who wanted to leave their same-sex partner but were afraid to leave the security of the known for the insecurity of the unknown. It reminds me of a discussion in the Bible about what you have to be willing to do to follow what you know God intends for you — it might cost you everything of worldly value. One woman wrote Lisa explaining that she had wanted to take her child and leave her abusive same-sex partner but had no idea about how she would provide for herself and her child if she had to start all over. After staying longer than she should have in the relationship, she finally realized that, despite the fear and risk of the unknown, she needed to leave in order to protect her child. She was willing to leave it all behind to do what she knew in her heart was right. She later told Lisa,

> "I let her have everything we both had in our names. I gave it all to her: the cars, SUV, the boats, computers, and the savings. It was hard but God told me to let go of all the stuff even though I bought it myself. She never worked. My home and car and van still are mine but thousand upon thousand went out the door with her, even our savings. But it's over!!! Praise God it's over!"

If you are involved in a same-sex relationship or struggling with same-sex attractions and ever had a doubt about whether this was right or whether there was something better for your life, please know that God does have a better plan for your life. He wants you to know Him in a way so that for the first time in your life you could feel wholly accepted and loved, unconditionally. Regardless of the choices you've made in life, He has a better plan for your life. That doesn't mean it will be easy or without difficult decisions. It does mean, however, that you will be living a life that your Creator, who knew you even before you were born, specifically created you for. Psalm 139:13.

If you have a child, the decision to leave the relationship can be even harder. From our earthly, human perspective it's harder to leave because we want the reassurance that we will be able to provide for our children, to put a roof over their heads, and to feed them. Leaving a same-sex relationship may mean you don't know how that will happen. Lisa has told me at least a dozen stories where during the years of the litigation, God literally provided her with food, money, a computer, and even a car at times when she didn't even know from where the next meal would come. She trusted that He would provide, and He did.

Before we take a closer look at Lisa's journey of healing, let me share a bit of my story with you to highlight that regardless of your background and what issues you are currently dealing with, we all share similar needs and struggles. I came to know Christ as my savior in July 1990 at the age of 20. That summer, God took me on a six week journey from the lowest point in my life, where life seemed hopeless and, frankly, because of all the things that had happened in my life and the lives of those I loved, I readily told people that God either did not exist or I hated him if He did. That summer, through lots of prayer, discussion, and unconditional love, a group of friends allowed God to use them to lead me to Christ. For me, some things were immediately changed in my life. Significantly, I went from feeling years of emptiness or worthlessness to instantly feeling a sense of peace and joy I'd never known. God also immediately changed my views on some things, giving me an understanding that whatever I believed needed to conform to His word. Thus, while I didn't really have a thorough understanding of the issues, God immediately transformed my beliefs on life and relationships: I went from pro-choice to pro-life overnight. I also immediately changed my views about marriage and relationships. To this day, I distinctly recall a conversation I had at the beginning of that summer, before I became a Christian, with one of my friends, where I explained that it was none of government's business to tell a loving same-sex couple that they couldn't marry or be together. Although my views on that issue also immediately changed once I became a Christian, it wasn't until years later that I truly grasped the importance of God's design for marriage.

Other things, however, were a process and are still a process today. If we stop and think a moment, we can all think of things we know God needs to still work on in us — for some it's bad language, sarcasm, or watching things we shouldn't; for others it's a short temper, or ... you fill in the blank. We know these are sin issues in our life and we make commitments over and over again to work on them and let God work in us in these areas, but don't see the immediate change that we might have seen in other areas. For addictions, it's the same. I've spoken to people who had an alcohol or drug addiction and God took the desires away overnight. For others, it's a day by day, moment by moment struggle to resist temptations, to identify the triggers in life and respond appropriately. "Coming out of homosexuality doesn't mean coming out of temptation."[47] Overcoming temptations is a daily, and sometimes a moment-by-moment, choice. Lisa's struggles were no different.

There are some issues in her life that God completely took away, others that God has worked on and the struggles have lessened, and others that continue to be a day to day struggle. A quote by Randy Thomas, Executive Vice President of Exodus International, is a great reminder for all of us when it comes to the issue of dealing with these various sin issues in our life. He explains that "the opposite of homosexuality is not heterosexuality — it's holiness."[48] Whatever our struggles in life with various sin issues, we should not be on a journey simply to rid ourselves of that sin issue — to use good language, to avoid pornography, etc. — but on a life-long journey in pursuit of holiness. As we progress down the path toward holiness, these other issues will take care of themselves. For example, if you fill your heart and mind with God's word, what flows out of your mouth will be consistent with God's word rather than inappropriate language. If you fill your heart and mind with movies and books that are full of language, morals, and images that do not honor God, then it should come as no surprise that bad language comes out of your mouth or that you struggle with lustful thoughts. We should seek to study God's character through His word and prayer to see our lives transformed through the process.

During the process, we need to have a proper understanding of holiness. Many of us tend to equate holiness to goodness and therefore deprive God of the opportunity to do amazing work in our lives. If we view goodness and holiness as synonymous then we tend to start comparing ourselves to others or where we are now to where we were a few years back. Thus, we start to tell ourselves that compared to my friends or neighbors, I live a pretty good life, which, translated, means we perceive ourselves to be further down the holiness path than others. Alternatively, we might look back and see how much

God has changed our lives, and think, again, that we have made good progress down the holiness path. Our standard of holiness, however, should be the all knowing, perfect God who spoke the heavens and earth into creation and who is the same today, tomorrow, and forever.[49] If that's our standard, we're never far enough down the path to holiness that we can take it easy or rest a bit. Nor should our pursuit of holiness be out of a sense of obligation. Rather, we should pursue holiness because we realize that all sin is against God and that it grieves Him to see us make poor choices; we should desire to make right choices because it pleases God.

Viewed in this perspective, you realize that the question isn't whether my bucket of thoughts and actions contain more good than bad (and thus I can "afford" to go see that movie, read that book, or engage in that conduct). Every choice we make sends us in one of two directions — on the road to holiness, through a choice that glorifies our Creator, or on the road away from Christ. There is no middle ground — no neutrality. James 4:4 explains that "anyone who chooses to be a friend of the world becomes an enemy of God." Therefore, as Timothy reminds us, we are to "[f]lee the evil desires of youth, and pursue righteousness, faith, love, and peace, along with those who call on the Lord out of a pure heart."[50] Paul instructs us in Colossians 3:5 to "Put to death, therefore, whatever belongs to your earthly nature: sexual immorality, impurity, lust, evil desires and greed, which is idolatry." Through Christ's strength we can choose to pursue holiness.

Lisa's journals highlight the daily nature of the struggle to overcome her addictions. One thing that was eye opening for me was the significant and direct way life events are triggers for the addictions. I guess if I had thought about it, I shouldn't have been surprised. After all, whatever our sin issues, there is usually something that triggers the improper response by us — having a bad day at work will lead some to be short tempered; being depressed over a loved one will lead some to console themselves with alcohol; hating life and wanting a way out will cause some to respond by using drugs to escape from reality. Lisa's addictions to cutting, pornography, and same-sex attractions were no different. In fact, one book she read shortly after she decided to leave the homosexual lifestyle explained the importance of identifying the triggers to the feelings that tempt us to sin.[51] For Lisa, she knew what the triggers were and sought God's grace, sometimes moment by moment, to overcome the temptations.

At times, Lisa struggled daily to overcome temptations, to resist giving in to what the feelings of loneliness made her want to do. Some days were good, some were not. She rejoiced when days and weeks would pass without having given in to any of the temptations. She also discussed repeatedly the direct link between her thought life and how much time she spent in prayer and Bible reading. At one point she realized that if she didn't read the Bible at least three times a day and pray throughout the day, the temptations would creep into her mind. But when she spent that time with God, getting to know His truth, His character, His promises, and His purpose for her life, she wasn't tempted. Lisa's two primary triggers were loneliness and anger. When she felt isolated from others, with no one who truly understood her or loved her unconditionally, she would be more tempted to give in to a fleshly, worldly way to attempt to fill the loneliness. Similarly, when she was angry about her life circumstances, she would be tempted to give in to the lure of past addictions.

Lisa's daily struggles and times of incredible fellowship with God reminds me of an old hymn, *Turn Your Eyes Upon Jesus*.

> O soul, are you weary and troubled?
> No light in the darkness you see?
> There's light for a look at the Savior
> And life more abundant and free!

> Through death into life everlasting
> He passed, and we follow Him there;
> Over us sin no more hath dominion-
> For more than conquerors we are!

> His word shall not fail you-He promised;
> Believe him, and all will be well;

Then go to a world that is dying,
His perfect salvation to tell!

Chorus:
Turn your eyes upon Jesus,
Look full in His wonderful face,
And the things of earth will grow strangely dim
In the light of his glory and grace.

What is so important to understand is that God's grace is sufficient to cover over any sin, regardless of how horrible or unforgiveable we think it is. Each one of us was uniquely created by God and He has a plan and a purpose for our life that does *not* include living a life of emptiness and hopelessness. We each have the opportunity, through Jesus Christ's sacrificial death on the cross, to live a new life where we are not in bondage to our sinful desires or past choices. Satan would like nothing more than to convince us of the lie that there is no hope for change in our lives.

Chapter Eight

How Homosexuality Impacts Our Children

During the past seven years, I have heard and seen a lot of things that break my heart. One of the most difficult for me to grasp is when people tell me that while they are personally opposed to same-sex marriage they don't see why the issue has to be a top election issue or how legalizing same-sex relationships will in any way hurt them. I don't necessarily blame them for feeling this way since many of our churches have failed to teach us why this issue is so important, the media glamorizes the lifestyle, and schools tell our children that homosexuality is normal and healthy. I also understand that people are extremely busy and have to choose which battles to fight. It is my hope that in sharing my heart in this book you will see why I truly believe that this issue impacts everyone, and why I pray daily that everyone who believes in family and freedom will engage in the war that has been waged against the traditional family. I'd like to spend the next few pages discussing how homosexuality impacts our children. As one prominent lesbian author wrote, "It's the first fact of civilization, whoever captures the kids owns the future."[52] That fact became very clear for me when I saw Rosie O'Donnell interviewed on Oprah about her HBO documentary "A Family is a Family is a Family: A Rosie O'Donnell Celebration."

During the interview, there was a clip of Rosie with her then seven year old daughter Vivienne. (Actually, Vivienne is the biological child of Rosie's former partner Kelli Carpenter, but the child calls Rosie "mom" and her biological mother, "Kel."). Rosie is talking with Vivienne as they do arts and crafts together. Rosie tells Vivienne that most people have a "mommy and a daddy in your class, but you have two mommies." She then asks Vivienne, "Did you ever want a daddy?" Vivienne just shakes her head. Rosie prompts her, "No? I think a daddy might be fun."

In that short video clip, it's clear that a sweet little child has been raised to believe it's perfectly normal to have two moms and that a little girl doesn't need the love and care of a father. What we teach to, and model for, our children directly impacts what they believe — for good and for bad. As Christians the Bible is quite clear that God's standard for marriage is one man and one woman united for life. We don't have the authority to change His standards or to call "good" that which He has called sin. It is important that we spend some time learning about who is in the battle to capture our children and what it is they are teaching them.

When I speak publicly on this issue, I like to start the discussion with a bit of a disclaimer. Often, I'm accused of being homophobic or hating homosexuals. I think the first accusation is pretty quickly dispensed with — I certainly do not fear homosexuals. Maybe there are those out there who are homophobic, but I haven't actually met one yet. Unfortunately, I have met those who hate homosexuals, but I am not among them. Rather, God has laid on my heart a compassion for those struggling with same-sex attractions. Just as my heart breaks when I hear the painful testimony of a woman who regrets the abortion she had as a young woman because she was deceived to believe that she had no choice in life but to kill her unborn baby, my heart breaks for those who are deceived to believe that they were born gay and have no choice but to live a life that is emotionally, physically, and spiritually unhealthy. Just as there are people dedicated to keeping the truth from the woman who thinks she has no choice but to kill her unborn child, there are those in society who are actively deceiving our youth about homosexuality by lying to our children and encouraging them to make destructive life choices.

There is a concerted, ongoing effort around the Nation to teach our children that same-sex attractions are normal and that sexual exploration should begin at a young age. Here are several recent examples:[53]

- In June 2010, a private school in New York City for students with autism staged a production of La Cage aux Folles, requiring male students as young as ten years old to dress up as girls.[54]

- In October 2008, eight first graders took a field trip to San Francisco City Hall for the "wedding" of their teacher and her lesbian partner; public school administrators called the field trip "a teachable moment."[55]

- A public school nurse in California explained in an interview that as part of the school's efforts during Gay Pride Month, the school had created the Rainbow Café where each day students could discuss a different topic related to sexuality and LGBT (Lesbian, Gay, Bisexual, and Transgender) issues. To encourage attendance by "kids who wouldn't be exposed to this kind of programming," teachers were encouraged to give extra credit to students who participated.[56]

- The Maine Human Rights Commission ruled that a school district unlawfully discriminated against a transgendered fifth grade student by denying the boy access to the girls' restrooms in the school. Initially, the school permitted the boy to use the girls' restrooms but required him to use a single-stall faculty bathroom after boys began to harass him for using the girls' restrooms.[57] Unhappy with that compromise, the parents filed a discrimination complaint against the school and won. The school now must allow the boy to use the girls' restroom and take all necessary steps to keep the child safe. In March 2010, the Commission held a public hearing on its proposal to require all schools in Maine to permit transgendered students to use the restroom of their choice, regardless of whether they are boys or girls.

● One organization that has dedicated itself to LGBT issues in public schools is GLSEN (Gay, Lesbian, Straight Education Network). Kevin Jennings, founder of GLSEN, was appointed by President Obama to lead the "safe school" efforts at the Department of Education.[58] Soon after the appointment, we learned that while Jennings was a teacher he failed to report to authorities that a 15 year old student told him of a sexual relationship with an older man.[59] Instead, Jennings apparently encouraged the boy to use a condom.[60] Ironically, Jennings was put in charge of making our schools safe. As part of GLSEN's efforts to eradicate what it describes as "homophobia" and "heterosexism" in schools, it creates curriculum for teachers to use in schools, encourages students to participate in several special days throughout the school year (including Ally Week, No Name Calling Week, TransAction Day, and Day of Silence), and promotes formation of the now more than 4,700 gay-straight alliance clubs in schools around the country.[61] In one of its educational resources, GLSEN discusses "institutional heterosexism" in schools.[62] GLSEN defines heterosexism as "the belief that homosexuality is 'wrong' or 'less than [heterosexuality],'" the belief that "heterosexuality is 'better' or more 'normal [than homosexuality],'" or "the assumption that the gender roles today's society assigns to males and females are 'natural' and 'right.'"[63] "Heterosexism is not a replacement for homophobia. Rather it is a broader term that does not imply the same level of hatred, and which can describe seemingly innocent thoughts and behavior on the belief that heterosexuality is the norm."[64] In other words, GLSEN wants our schools to believe that referring to moms and dads when discussing family is heterosexist because it perpetuates stigma against those in same-sex relationships.

● GLSEN's various "special days" all have the goal of gaining wider public acceptance for those with same-sex sexual attractions or gender identity confusion. Ally Week takes place in October and encourages all students to become allies against anti-LGBT discrimination and harassment.[65] GLSEN hosts an Education Allies Network in support of the day and offers educators a Safe Space kit.[66] On the Day of Silence, in April each year, students are encouraged to remain silent all day and distribute cards to encourage other students to end the silence about the alleged anti-LGBT discrimination taking place in the schools.[67] While everyone should oppose harassment in our schools, GLSEN goes much further. By recognizing these "special days" devoted to LGBT issues, it normalizes same-sex attractions in the minds of our children.

A fairly recent day created by GLSEN is TransAction Day, which is celebrated in February each year. It is a "national day to encourage dialogue about gender, gender roles and the full range of gender identities, and to advocate for inclusive, safe schools for all students." GLSEN makes a variety of resources available to students and teachers, including materials entitled "Beyond the Binary" and "Bending the Mold."[68] One of the resources also includes a two page document entitled "Gender Terminology."[69] Some of the defined terms are: "Genderism: Related to sexism, but is the systematic belief that people need to conform to the gender role assigned to them based on a gender binary system which includes only female and male. This is a form of institutionalized discrimination as well as individually demonstrated prejudice." In other words, children are told that it is discriminatory to believe that children should be encouraged to live consistently with their biological sex. "Butch" is used to describe "people of all genders and sexes who act and dress in stereotypically masculine ways." The Gender Terminology document also explains that we need to begin using "gender-neutral pronouns" to avoid discrimination. Instead of "he" or "she," we are encouraged to use "zie;" instead of his or her, we are encouraged to use "hir." GLSEN encourages teachers to use the instructional materials in classrooms around the Nation.

- Another organization that targets our children, PFLAG (Parents, Families and Friends of Lesbians and Gays), markets a brochure called "Be Yourself" to students.[70] In it, PFLAG explains to students that "One or two sexual experiences with someone of the same sex may not mean you're gay.... Your school years are a time of figuring out what works for you, and crushes and experimentation are often part of that."[71] It actively encourages students to experiment with their sexuality in their youth.[72] PFLAG also tells students that being gay, lesbian, bisexual, or transgender is "as natural" as "being straight ... it's as healthy to be gay, lesbian or bisexual as to be straight — no matter what some people might tell you."[73]

- In one upstate New York school district, when a male high school teacher returned after summer break dressing as a female (as part of his transition period before having sex reassignment surgery), administrators showed students a slideshow presentation entitled Gender Identity Awareness (GID).[74] It told students that a person with GID "wake[s] up every day in the wrong body."[75] As a result, administrators told students that they were to "respect all people's differences," including addressing the male teacher as "Ms."[76]

Despite parental objections to this type of values training, schools continue to condition our children to accept these harmful and misleading messages because traditional legal remedies have not posed any real obstacle to schools' efforts. In many states, parents have a statutory right to opt children out of certain objectionable curriculum. However, the laws are not broadly written to permit a student to be excused from any materials parents find objectionable, but tend to deal only with sex education.[77] Very few states require that parents be notified that they have the right to opt their children out.[78] Thus, while parents have the legal right to opt their children out, they might not even know that they have that right or that the school is teaching potentially objectionable materials. Of the states with an opt out law, only four permit parents to opt out based on religious or moral beliefs. Three of the states with an opt out law only permit students to opt out of STD/HIV instruction — not sex education.

No state permits parents to opt their children out of discussion or instruction about same-sex attractions or gender identity issues that is not part of a sex or STD/HIV education class. In other words, parents do not have any right to opt children out of other classroom instruction or discussion that seeks to normalize sexual and gender identity confusion. Thus, if the history, literature, sociology, psychology, or science teacher wishes to discuss the issue with students, then parents have no legal right to opt their children out under state law. Parents have fewer rights under federal law. No federal law grants parents the right to opt children out of any curriculum in public schools. As a result, parents have resorted to claims that a state's refusal to permit an opt out violates the parents' fundamental right to direct the education and upbringing of their children.

The United States Supreme Court long has protected parents' liberty interest in making decisions concerning their child's upbringing. A parent's fundamental right has been described as "perhaps the oldest of the fundamental liberty interests."[79] The Supreme Court has explained that because "[t]he child is not the mere creature of the state,"[80] "[i]t is cardinal ... that the custody, care and nurture of the child resides first in the parents, whose primary function and freedom include preparation for obligations the state can neither supply nor hinder."[81]

The importance placed upon the relationship between the child and fit, legal parents, is also apparent in the higher standard of proof required before the state can substantially interfere with the parents' constitutional rights.[82] "[T]he interest of a parent in the companionship, care, custody, and management of his or her children 'come(s) to this Court with a momentum for respect lacking when appeal is made to liberties which derive merely from shifting economic arrangements.'"[83] "Choices about marriage, family life and the upbringing of children are among associational rights this Court has ranked as of basic importance in our society, rights sheltered by the Fourteenth Amendment against the state's unwarranted usurpation, disregard, or disrespect."[84]

The state's interest in caring for the child of natural or adoptive parents is *de minimis* if the parents are fit parents.[85]

What appears to be strong protection of parents' rights to decide when and how their children will be exposed to comprehensive sex education, including instruction on sexual and gender identity issues, evaporates in the face of the broad discretion that the courts have given to schools. The United States Supreme Court has explained that schools are tasked with educating our youth with the "fundamental values necessary to the maintenance of a democratic political system.... [S]chools must teach by example the shared values of a civilized social order. The schools, as instruments of the state, may determine that the essential lessons of civil, mature conduct cannot be conveyed in a school that tolerates lewd, or offensive speech and conduct...."[86] In two other cases, the Court further explained,

> "a sound education 'is the very foundation of good citizenship. Today it is a principal instrument in awakening the child to cultural values, in preparing him for later professional training, and in helping him to adjust normally to his environment.' We have recognized the public schools as a most vital civic institution for the preservation of a democratic system of government ... and as the primary vehicle for transmitting the values on which our society rests.... In sum, education has a fundamental role in maintaining the fabric of our society.'"[87]

The Supreme Court has given "broad discretionary powers" for schools to teach whatever values *they* deem appropriate.[88]

The obvious question becomes what happens when the school's values instruction conflicts with the beliefs of the student's parents. Several federal appellate courts have concluded that the state, not the parents, will prevail in the conflict as long as the school has a legitimate reason for its instruction. One court stated it this way:

> "It is axiomatic that competing constitutional claims are found in a school setting. Students, teachers, parents, administra-

tors, and the state as *parens patriae*, all have legitimate rights to further their respective goals. Sometimes these rights clash. Thus, while there is a constitutional right to freedom of religion, it is not absolute and may be circumscribed by a compelling state interest."[89]

In deciding between the two competing interests, courts have decided that the school's obligation to educate trumps parental rights. As a result, "parental requests that their children be exempted from a part of the general public school programs have been frequently denied."[90] The courts have explained that when "parents choose to enroll their children in public schools, they cannot demand that the school program be tailored to meet their individual preferences, even those based on religion or a right of privacy."[91] A review of a few cases in this area highlights the consequences of the broad discretion granted to school boards.

In *Brown v. Hot, Sexy and Safer Productions, Inc.*,[92] the parents of two Massachusetts high school students claimed that public school officials violated their right to direct the upbringing of their children when the district sponsored a mandatory school AIDS awareness assembly that featured sexually explicit language and sexually explicit skits with several students selected from the audience. The students alleged that during the assembly, presenters advocated and approved oral sex, masturbation, homosexual sexual activity, and premarital sex.[93] In rejecting the parents' claim that the instruction violated their parental rights, the court explained that a parent's right involves "choosing a specific educational program — whether it be religious instruction at a private school or instruction in a foreign language.... [T]he state does not have the power to 'standardize its children' or 'foster homogenous people' by completely foreclosing the opportunity of individuals and groups to choose a different path of education."[94] Parents do not, however, have a "right to dictate the curriculum at the public school to which they have chosen to send their children.... If all parents had a fundamental constitutional right to dictate individually what the schools teach their children, the schools would be forced to cater a curriculum for each student whose parents had genuine moral disagreements with the school's choice of subject matter."[95]

In another case from Massachusetts, the state's highest court was asked whether it violated parents' rights for the school to provide condoms to juniors and seniors without parental notice or a right to opt their children out of the program. Holding that the "[p]ublic education of children is unquestionably entrusted to the control, management, and discretion of State and local communities," the court concluded that the condom distribution program did not violate the parents' constitutional rights.[96] It explained that,

> "we discern no coercive burden on the plaintiffs' parental liberties in this case. No classroom participation is required of students. Condoms are available to students who request them and, in high school, may be obtained from vending machines. The students are not required to seek out and accept the condoms, read the literature accompanying them, or participate in counseling regarding their use.... For their part, the plaintiff parents are free to instruct their children not to participate.... Although exposure to condom vending machines and to the program itself may offend the moral and religious sensibilities of plaintiffs, mere exposure to programs offered at school does not amount to an unconstitutional interference with parental liberties without the existence of some compulsory aspect of the program."[97]

The Ninth Circuit Court of Appeals also rejected a claim that parents' rights were violated when their elementary-age school children in California were exposed to sexual questions in a questionnaire that parents were told was designed to assess trauma resulting from the terrorist attacks on 9/11.[98] Some of the questions asked the elementary school students to rate various activities on a scale from "never" to "almost all of the time." Those questions included the following: (i) touching my private parts too much, (ii) thinking about having sex, (iii) thinking about touching other people's private parts, (iv) thinking about sex when I don't want to, (v) not trusting people because they might want sex, and (vi) can't stop thinking about sex.[99] The Ninth Circuit held that the parents' rights were not violated because parents have no rights concerning what their children are taught in school. Echoing the rationale of the court in *Brown v. Hot, Sexy and Safer Productions, Inc.*, the Ninth Circuit held that,

> "once parents make the choice as to which school their children will attend, their fundamental right to control the education of their children is, at the least, substantially diminished. The constitution does not vest parents with the authority to interfere with the public school's decision as to how it will provide information to its students or what information it will provide, in its classrooms or otherwise....'While parents may have a fundamental right to decide *whether* to send their children to a public school, they do not have a fundamental right generally to direct how a public school teaches their child. Whether it is the school curriculum, the hours of the school day, school discipline, the timing and content of examinations, the individuals hired to teach at the school, the extracurricular activities offered at the school.... these issues of public education are generally committed to the control of state and local authorities.'"[100]

What make these two decisions particularly disturbing is that in both instances the schools violated state laws mandating that parents receive notice in advance of such events that specifically told them (i) about the proposed instruction and that (ii) they have the right to opt their children out of the instruction. In other words, the court found no violation of parental rights despite the fact that the schools violated state laws that expressly gave parents an opt out right.

A federal district court in Florida similarly rejected a claim by parents that the school's promotion of a telephone counseling line with recorded messages on sensitive topics violated parental rights.[101] The Link Line provided recorded messages on a variety of topics, including masturbation, sexuality, pregnancy, stress management, and drug use. Anyone could access the recorded messages. Dade County Schools distributed the phone number throughout their schools, displayed posters advertising Link Line and, on occasion, teachers played Link Line messages in their classroom. The court concluded that the parents' rights were not violated because the "Link Line messages evince an attempt to instill students with purely secular values and equip them with the necessary tools to arrive an informed decisions."[102]

In yet another decision arising out of an incident in Massachusetts schools, the court reaffirmed that parents have no constitutional right to dictate what their children are taught. As part of the Lexington school system's effort to educate its students to understand and respect gays, lesbians, and their families, teachers read to first grade students a book entitled "King and King," which is a story where a prince marries another prince.[103] When parents learned that teachers read the book to their children, they asked the school for a right to opt their children out of future instruction that teaches acceptance of same-sex relationships. The court concluded that a Massachusetts law, which gives parents the right to exempt children from any curriculum that *primarily* involves human sexual education or human sexuality issues, does not cover the type of classroom discussion that the plaintiffs' children encountered.

In rejecting the parents' constitutional claims, the court articulated an extremely broad grant of authority to the public schools:

> "In essence, under the Constitution public schools are entitled to teach anything that is reasonably related to the goals of preparing students to become engaged and productive citizens in our democracy. Diversity is a hallmark of our nation. It is increasingly evident that our diversity includes differences in sexual orientation.... It is reasonable for public educators to teach elementary school students about individuals with different sexual orientations and about various forms of families, including those with same-sex parents, in an effort to eradicate the effects of past discrimination and, in

the process, to reaffirm our nation's constitutional commitment to promoting mutual respect among members of our
diverse society. In addition, it is reasonable for those educators to find that teaching young children to understand and
respect differences in sexual orientation will contribute to
an academic environment in which students who are gay,
lesbian, or the children or same-sex parents will be comfortable and, therefore, better able to learn."[104]

The court explained that if the school were required to permit parents to
opt children out of discussions concerning homosexuality, "[a]n exodus from
the classroom ... could send the message that gays, lesbians, and the children
of same-sex parents are inferior and, therefore, have a damaging effect on those
students."[105] "[T]he very purpose of schools is the preparation of individuals
for participation as citizens and therefore local education officials may attempt
to promote civic virtues that awaken the child to cultural values. Schools are
expected to transmit civic values.... [T]he state is expected to teach civic
values as part of its preparation of students for citizenship."[106] "One of the
most fundamental of those values is mutual respect.... Students today must
be prepared for citizenship in a diverse society."[107]

The court also was quite clear that schools are tasked with changing the
minds of our children on the issue of homosexuality, even if such instruction
is contrary to parents' religious beliefs on the issue. "A key to changing a mind
is to produce a shift in the individual's mental representations. As it is difficult
to change attitudes and stereotypes after they have developed, it is reasonable
for public schools to attempt to teach understanding and respect for gays and
lesbians to young students...."[108] The problem is that what schools call tolerance most of us call silencing all those who oppose a radical redefinition of
family and marriage.

If the 2009 Report of the American Psychological Association (APA)
Task Force on Appropriate Therapeutic Responses to Sexual Orientation is
any indication of what our children will be taught in the years to come, we
have reason to be concerned. The APA is the organization that declassified

homosexuality as a mental disorder in 1973, and then later declassified pedophilia and sadomasochism as disorders except to the extent the person feels guilt or shame about their conduct. The task force, which consisted of medical professionals who all were either openly homosexual or actively involved in advancing homosexual causes, wrote a report on its beliefs about whether it is appropriate to treat those with unwanted same-sex. If schools rely on the APA's conclusions, as many schools tend to do, here is what we can expect our children to be taught in school:

- "Same-sex sexual attractions, behavior, and orientation per se are normal and positive variants of human sexuality," without any discussion of the increased physical and mental health risks associated with the homosexual lifestyle.[109]

- "Gay men, lesbians, and bisexual individuals form stable, committed relationships and families that are equivalent to heterosexual relationships and families in essential respects," without explaining that there are no solid studies to document that claim and, in fact, that many sources have discussed how "monogamy" in homosexual relationships means having one steady partner while engaging in many sexual relationships on the side.[110]

- A student who expresses a desire to want to resist same-sex attractions will be told that his feelings are based on stigma the student feels from religious beliefs of his parents or friends and that rather than attempt to change his same-sex attractions he should change his friends or religion.[111]

- Students should explore their sexual identity "by accepting homosexuality and bisexuality as normal and positive variants of human sexual orientation"[112] and that any attempts to resist or change their same-sex attractions could be harmful.[113]

Unfortunately, the direction the Supreme Court has taken is to give schools wide discretion to decide what values it wants to teach while stripping parents of the ability to prevent their children from being exposed to beliefs and values that undermine their own. Contrary to what some think, the solution is *not* to move schools in the direction of teaching curriculum from a value-neutral perspective. The reality is that someone's values always will be taught in school. It is impossible for a school system to teach all of its curriculum in a moral vacuum. The curriculum and classroom instruction are infused with the values and beliefs of those who establish the curriculum and instruct the children. Certainly, schools could steer clear of sex education to avoid obvious differences of opinion on the controversial subject but, as we will see below, the issues arise in other classes, including literature, history, science, and social studies. Schools and teachers decide which books to read, what parts of history to discuss, which view on origins to teach, and what role government has in ensuring "equal rights."

The argument that schools should refrain from values instruction also ignores the fact that from the outset schools were viewed as a means to transmit important moral values to the next generation. The founders of this Nation understood that an educated citizenry was vital to our success as a Nation and that a vital component of that education was proper morals training. The problem today, however, is that as a Nation we have strayed so far from Judeo-Christian moral values that public schools now teach values that directly contradict those our founders understood were necessary to the preservation of the republic.

President George Washington reminded us in his 1796 Farewell Address that there are two indispensable supports to the political prosperity of a republic: religion and morality.[114] He also made clear that a particular type of morality was essential to the Nation's continued success — morality based on Judeo-Christian principles. Benjamin Rush, a signer of the Declaration of Independence, echoed that sentiment, connecting education and morals with the preservation of liberty: "the only foundation for a useful education in a republic is to be laid in Religion. Without this there can be no virtue, and without virtue there can be no liberty, and liberty is the object and life of all republican governments."[115]

As a result, Noah Webster cautioned young people in 1834 about the type of leaders we should elect:

> "When you become entitled to exercise the right of voting for public officers, let it be impressed on your mind that God commands you to choose for rules, just men who will rule in the fear of God. The preservation of a republican government depends on the faithful discharge of this duty; if the citizens neglect their duty, and place unbridled men in office, the government will soon be corrupted; laws will be made, not for the public good, so much as for selfish or local purposes; corrupt or incompetent men will be appointed to execute the laws; the public revenues will be squandered on unworthy men; and the rights of the citizens will be violated or disregarded. If a republican government fails to secure public prosperity and happiness, it must be because the citizens neglect the divine commands, and elect bad men to make and administer the laws."[116]

From the very beginning of our Nation, education was viewed as an essential means to properly prepare citizens in our political system. The United States Supreme Court has explained that:

> "The 'American people have always regarded education and [the] acquisition of knowledge as matters of supreme importance.' We have recognized 'the public schools as a most vital civic institution for the preservation of a democratic system of government,' and as the primary vehicle for transmitting 'the values on which our society rests. [A]s ... pointed out early in our history, ... some degree of education is necessary to prepare citizens to participate effectively and intelligently in our open political system if we are to preserve freedom and independence.' And these historic 'perceptions of the public schools as inculcating fundamental values necessary to

the maintenance of a democratic political system have been confirmed by the observations of social scientists.' In addition, education provides the basic tools by which individuals might lead economically productive lives to the benefit of us all. In sum, education has a fundamental role in maintaining the fabric of our society."[117]

As Alexis de Tocqueville traveled around America for nine months in 1831, studying our political system as a possible model for post-revolutionary France, he also noted the importance of an educated citizenry, particularly an education firmly grounded in proper morals.[118] While it seems as though everyone would accept the proposition that values must be taught to the next generation, delegating to public schools the authority to transmit *proper* values raises unique concerns in our Nation at this time.

Language from a 1986 United States Supreme Court opinion swings the door wide open for schools to inculcate those values that the *school district* determines appropriate. In *Bethel v. Fraser*, a school district suspended a high school student for a sexually graphic metaphor he used in a nominating speech he made at a school assembly. In upholding the school district's decision to sanction the student for his speech, the Court offered this explanation:

> "Surely it is a highly appropriate function of public school education to prohibit the use of vulgar and offensive terms in public discourse. Indeed, the 'fundamental values necessary to the maintenance of a democratic political system' disfavor the use of terms of debate highly offensive or highly threatening to others. Nothing in the Constitution prohibits the states from insisting that certain modes of expression are inappropriate and subject to sanctions. *The inculcation of these values is truly the 'work of the schools.' The determination of what manner of speech in the classroom or in school assembly is inappropriate properly rests with the school board.* The process of educating our youth for citizenship in public schools is

not confined to books, the curriculum, and the civics class; *schools must teach by example the shared values of a civilized social order.* Consciously or otherwise, teachers — and indeed the older students — demonstrate the appropriate form of civil discourse and political expression by their conduct and deportment in and out of class. Inescapable, like parents, they are role models. *The schools, as instruments of the state, may determine that the essential lessons of civil, mature conduct cannot be conveyed in a school that tolerates lewd, indecent, or offensive speech and conduct....*"[119]

While many would agree that the student's speech was inappropriate and the school acted appropriately in suspending the student, it raises an obvious question concerning sex education, diversity training, and tolerance for all choices concerning sexuality in our schools today: whether the broad grant of discretion to schools includes the authority to inculcate values based on misinformation that puts students at risk. Namely, whether schools, in the name of tolerance, diversity, school safety, or health education can teach our children that same-sex sexual attractions are normal and healthy and that parents should foster a child's desire to explore his or her gender identity.

For those of you who live in states that permit "marriage" between same-sex couples, or allow them to enter into some relationship equivalent to marriage, you have probably already faced issues with what is taught in the schools, most likely losing many of the battles because the state believes it has some obligation to train children to accept homosexuality as normal. For others, you might think that these things wouldn't be taught in your schools. More than one-third of the states, however, already have laws or policies in place that prohibit discrimination in schools based on sexual orientation. In many more, individual teachers, guidance counselors, and local school boards, encourage children to accept homosexuality as a positive lifestyle choice to explore. The 2007 National School Climate Survey by GLSEN (Gay Lesbian Straight Education Network) indicates that 12.7% of LGBT (lesbian, gay, bisexual, and transgendered) students surveyed reported that LGTB-related topics were taught in school.[120] Of that percentage, 82.7% reported that LGBT people or events were positively portrayed.[121] Those same students stated that LGBT issues are not limited to sex education courses but are taught across the curriculum, including history, literature, science, math, gym, and foreign languages.[122]

As Lisa's story demonstrates, what she learned and experienced during childhood dramatically impacted her adult life. As a teacher and a mom, she promised to be a positive role model, encouraging children to live a life pleasing to their Creator. Lisa understood the battle that is taking place for the hearts, minds, and souls of our children.

In a September 2009 e-mail, Lisa shared with me:

> "This battle is not only about Isabella and me — it is about parents' rights everywhere in the nation.... Isabella is a political hostage and is being used by the gay agenda to push their agenda of gay marriage. They say and have said in the past in regard to gay marriage that it will not hurt anyone. Well, they are wrong — a little seven year old girl is being hurt — and they want to rip her away from her biological mom (me) and give her to a legal stranger.... We are still a Christian Nation, and I believe that it is a Christian's duty to stand for what is right in God's eyes. I still put my trust in God and am blessed that He has been and still is with me every step of the way during this almost six years of litigation."

Chapter Nine

Understanding How the Homosexual Rights Movement Affects You and Your Loved Ones

While the battle over the minds and hearts of the next generation in itself demonstrates the urgency of the ongoing cultural war, a few examples outside the school context highlight how the homosexual rights movement directly threatens our First Amendment freedoms. Before turning to those cases, I need to stress that there will be a winner and a loser in this war. As Lisa explained in a September 2009 e-mail, "gay marriage is not a win-win situation. One side, and one side only, gets their rights and the other side loses their rights. As we've seen lately, the Christian has faced a series of losses. A loss for Christian values means we lose our liberties, including our inalienable rights to live out our religious beliefs."

Chai Feldblum, a professor of law at Georgetown Law Center whose 2009 appointment by President Obama to serve as a commissioner on the Equal Employment Opportunity Commission was confirmed in December 2010, makes the same point very clearly for us. She states that when religious liberties collide with homosexual rights, it's a "zero-sum game," which she explains to mean that as one side gains, the other side correspondingly loses.[123] President Obama, in a speech before the homosexual advocacy group, Human Rights Campaign, in October 2009, also depicted the battle as having a winner and a loser. He took the side of fighting for those who seek governmental approval for the homosexual lifestyle and characterized the majority of Americans who oppose normalizing sexual immorality as people "who hold fast to outworn arguments and old attitudes." I think too often we believe that there is room for a neutral compromise. We forget, however, that every compromise necessarily involves giving up some of our freedom.

We've learned in the past few years that the mantra of "tolerance" means tolerance for everything except that which the political correctness police deem intolerant — conveying the truth in love about homosexuality is at the top of the list of that which cannot be tolerated. More importantly, we need to remember that the leading homosexual activist organizations don't want compromise, they want complete victory. What does that victory look like? The pages that follow will hopefully give you a glimpse of the take no prisoners approach of the homosexual activist organizations. Let's start with the area of counseling.

Counseling

In 1973, homosexuality was declassified as a mental disorder. The American Psychological Association ("APA") then embraced the "gay rights" movement. The APA describes itself as "a scientific and professional organization that represents psychology in the United States." It controls the majority of publications in the mental health arena and represents to the public what it characterizes as the "mainstream" in the mental health profession. At the time homosexuality was removed from the DSM (Diagnostic and Statistical Manual of Mental Disorders), no one publicly admitted that the decision was politically motivated. Now, years later, the task force created to report on therapies related to same-sex attractions has finally admitted the political influences behind the decision.[124] Since 1973, and particularly in recent years, there has been an organized effort to prevent mental health providers from counseling patients that they have a choice about whether to live a homosexual lifestyle.

A recent report by the APA task force reached some startling conclusions concerning therapy designed to treat those with unwanted same-sex attractions. In August 2009, the task force, comprised of six members who are active in homosexual causes, issued its report entitled the Report of the American Psychological Association Task Force on Appropriate Therapeutic Responses to Sexual Orientation. All doctors who held a contrary belief concerning same-sex attractions were rejected for membership on the task force, despite well-established credentials.[125] After stating their belief that there isn't enough scientific evidence to reach a conclusion on whether efforts to change sexual orientation are effective, the task force concluded that "same-sex sexual attractions, behavior, and orientations per se are normal and positive variants of human sexuality" and that clients should be dissuaded from seeking therapy to deal with unwanted same-sex attractions.[126] The point is worth repeating.

Although the APA doesn't believe that there yet is enough evidence to decide if therapy is effective to help someone who desires to resist same-sex attractions, it takes the position that therapy to help people to resist same-sex attractions should be discouraged or banned. The task force claims that the reasons people seek to change their sexual orientation are societal and religious stigma. Stated differently, the APA maintains that only reason anyone would seek to change her same-sex attractions is because of what the APA considers intolerant religious views. Therefore, according to the task force, the mental health professional's obligation is to identify the underlying prejudices and stigma that have prompted the client's desire for change and then deconstruct those beliefs to make way for new ones that affirm a gay identity.[127]

NARTH (National Association for Research & Therapy of Homosexuality) was founded in 1992 to counter the APA's harmful actions. NARTH "upholds the rights of individuals with unwanted homosexual attraction to receive effective psychological care and the right of professionals to offer that care." NARTH explains its purpose and mission as follows:

> "The American Psychological Association has assumed an
> authority it cannot rightly claim. The group claims that science
> has somehow 'proven' that homosexuality and heterosexuality
> are qualitatively indistinguishable. Thus A.P.A. advocates in
> the political arena for a broad array of social policies—telling

our lawmakers that science supports, if not in fact mandates, gay marriage and adoption—as if any particular social policy could flow directly from the facts (from an 'is' to an 'ought') *without* an intervening philosophical judgment.

NARTH has responded to the mental-health professions' refusal to open itself up to socio-political diversity by advocating here for another view of sexuality and gender. No philosophical position—ours or the A.P.A.'s—is, *or can be*, scientifically 'neutral.'

NARTH's function is to provide psychological understanding of the cause, treatment and behavior patterns associated with homosexuality, within the boundaries of a civil public dialogue."

While NARTH is trying to ensure that those patients who want professional help to resist same-sex attractions can receive such help, the APA and ACA (American Counseling Association) seek to squelch those efforts. The ACA has concluded that it is wrong, and potentially harmful, to help people who desire to change their same-sex attractions.[128] Its ethical standards require counselors to inform patients who seek counseling for unwanted same sex attractions that there is no training for those who seek to counsel people with unwanted same-sex attractions, and that the treatment is not effective and even may cause harm.[129] As a result, in the sixteen states and the District of Columbia where the ACA Code of Ethics has been adopted into law, counselors could soon lose their licenses if they agree to counsel a client who seeks to resist same-sex attractions.[130] This is ironic, at best, given that the psychological community has protocols in place to assist patients who desire a sex change even though gender identity disorder (persistent belief that he was born the wrong sex that causes clinically significant distress in the person's life) is still classified as a mental disorder in the DSM.[131] Thus, while the APA and ACA seek to deny a patient's request for help to resist unwanted same-sex attractions, they are willing to assist a patient who desires to mutilate his body through hormone therapy and sex reassignment surgery. For anyone who saw the movie Expelled, all of this should sound very familiar. In the same way that universities across America silence those who follow the evidence toward the truth of a created universe (rather than one that evolved from a primordial blob, which blob itself inexplicably appeared out of nowhere), so too do the "mainstream" psychological associations seek to deny the evidence establishing that there is no "gay" gene and that people can choose to resist and overcome same-sex attractions. Truth is irrelevant; the agenda must be pursued despite evidence and common sense. Unfortunately, some courts rely on the misinformation provided by the APA and ACA.[132]

For example, a federal district court in Michigan recently upheld the decision of Eastern Michigan University to expel a student from a master's program in counseling whose religious beliefs prevented her from affirming the homosexual lifestyle of a client she had been assigned during her practicum.[133] When the student asked her supervisor whether the student could refer the client to another counselor, the supervisor began an investigation into the question of whether the student had violated the ACA policies. During a formal review, the student explained that she was willing to counsel homosexual patients on any issues other than relationship issues, which would require her to affirm their relationship. By a unanimous vote, she was dismissed from the program for having violated the ACA Code of Ethics. The District Court upheld that decision despite the student's first amendment challenge to the decision.

The Courts

With a basic understanding of the ideological battle that fuels the question of whether people are "born gay" and can change, perhaps it will be easier to understand how egregious (and ideologically motivated) some of the court decisions dealing with issues concerning same-sex attractions are. I hope, in the next few pages, to offer a glimpse of what is taking place in our courts as part of a concerted effort to gain full legal recognition for alternative family structures and to redefine our traditional understanding of who and what is a mother or father.

Let me start with a definition of an "activist judge." That phrase has been thrown around a lot in the past several years and obviously means different things to different people. For me, the definition is straightforward and is tied to the fact that the country is governed by the "rule of law," which simply means that we have federal and state constitutions and laws that all people, especially judges, are bound to follow, even if they do not like the law. There is one exception to this principle that judges are required to follow the law, even if they don't like it: judges are not bound to follow laws that violate the higher law — God's law.[134] Other than that exception, the only time a court should declare a law unconstitutional is if it plainly exceeds the authority granted to the legislature in the constitution. The reason is simple — the federal constitution represents a written contract signed by the Nation in 1789 and can only be modified in the way provided for in the contract. This last point is important — the contract (constitution) can be changed, but only by further written amendment approved by three-fourths of the states — not by the desires of 5 justices sitting on the Supreme Court (or, as I'll discuss later, one man serving as President). If a judge renders a decision that is not based on the rule of law but on his desires for what the law should be, then he is an activist judge because he is doing the job of the legislature. If the judge ignores the language of the constitution or creates rights that aren't actually in the constitution, then the judge is an activist judge.

There are a lot of activist judges in marriage and family litigation who have forgotten that they are only judges, not legislators, and make policy decisions and moral judgments that are to be made by the legislatures, not the judiciary. For example, *if* any branch of government has the authority to redefine marriage to mean the union of any two (or three or four) people, or to determine that two moms are just as good a mom and a dad, it would be the legislature, not the judiciary. Thankfully, there are still a good number of judges who know their job and the limitations upon their authority.

Let's begin with the subject of parental rights. As already discussed, in the context of public education, courts continue to chip away at any rights parents have concerning what is taught to their children in schools. The judiciary's tentacles reach much further under the guise of acting *parens patriae* or in the best interest of the child. *Parens patriae* is a latin phrase that means "parent of the country." Historically, it has applied to those instances where the government stepped in to care for an orphaned or abandoned child. It also is invoked to step in to help a child abused by her parents. Until recently, it was not understood to give courts authority to make child rearing decisions that contradict those of the fit parents. Courts rarely explain that they are invoking their *parens patriae* powers to overstep the decisions of the parents; instead, the decisions are couched in terms of the court's overarching obligation to do what is in the best interest of the child.

Anyone who has been around a child custody dispute has probably heard that phrase. Indeed, in all custody cases between parents the courts are charged to issue custody and visitation orders by determining what is in the best interest of the child. While I personally believe there must be a better system than the judicial system for determining custody and visitation in the divorce context, I at least understand the desire to have some "standard" to use in reaching the custody determination — we want the semblance of a reasoned decision on the issue when the two parents cannot decide and turn to a third party to make the decision. However, courts have no authority to make parental decisions for a child whose fit parents agree about the issue. Nevertheless, in the area of homeschooling, there is an effort afoot for judges to order parents to send their children to public or private school because judges, school officials, or social services employees believe homeschooling is not good for the child.

One Christian father recently found out that one court's decision of what is in the child's best interest means characterizing the father's Biblical beliefs as the "scariest" the judge has seen in more than twenty years and prohibiting the father from taking his son to church or engaging in any devotional exercise without the mother's permission. When the father subsequently read the Bible to his son, the court denied him all visitation.

Even more common is the courts' use of the best interest standard to completely redefine parentage. Although courts have described it in different ways, the result across the country has been the same — redefining parentage so that two moms or two dads are the same as a mom and a dad. Frequently, somewhere in the decision, the court mentions that it is better for the child to have two loving moms than to be intentionally left with a single parent, thus justifying the court's decision to declare a legal stranger to be the child's second parent. Let me introduce you to another Liberty Counsel client — Kristina S. In July 1997, Charisma and Kristina began dating in California and moved in together in August 1998.[135] In January 2002, they registered as domestic partners with the State of California.[136] Later that year, Kristina became pregnant by artificial insemination with sperm from an anonymous donor.[137] Her daughter was born in April 2003 and given a hyphenated last name, which was a combination of Charisma and Kristina's last names.[138] Charisma did not adopt Kristina's daughter even though California permitted second parent adoption by a same-sex partner.[139] In July 2003, when the baby was three months old, Kristina moved out of the home, taking her daughter with her.[140] On July 21, 2003, Kristina filed a termination of a domestic partnership.[141]

In May 2004, Charisma filed a petition in California to establish a parental relationship with Kristina's daughter.[142] In that petition, she stated that she and Kristina had decided to have a child together with the intention that they would both be the child's parents.[143] In October 2004, the trial court denied the petition, holding that under then-existing California law, Charisma lacked standing to bring the action under the Uniform Parentage Act.[144] In denying standing to Charisma, the trial court relied on three California Court of Appeals' decisions, each of which held that a former same-sex partner lacking a biological tie to a child could not establish a parent-child relationship with the child under the Uniform Parentage Act.[145]

Almost a year later, Kristina moved to Texas.[146] Two months later, in unrelated litigation, the California Supreme Court held *for the first time* that a child could have two mothers (without the use of second parent adoption) and that the *paternity*[147] presumption — used in determining a child's father — must "apply equally to women."[148] Specifically, the court held that California law should apply *to a woman* in a same-sex relationship the presumption that a man is the "natural father" of a child if "he receives the child into his home and openly holds out the child as his natural child."[149] In that decision, the court specifically stated its disapproval of the three Court of Appeals' decisions cited by the trial court in Charisma's case.[150] In light of the California Supreme Court ruling, the Court of Appeals remanded Charisma's case to determine, consistent with the California Supreme Court's August 2005 decision, whether Charisma is a presumed parent[151] and, if so, then whether this is an appropriate action in which to use scientific evidence to rebut the presumption that Charisma is a parent to Kristina's daughter.

By order dated December 27, 2006, which was more than one year after Kristina moved to Texas with her daughter, the California trial court declared Charisma to be a legal parent to Kristina's daughter pursuant to the paternity presumption.[152] The court cited three reasons, based on contested facts, for its conclusion that this was not "an appropriate action in which to rebut" the parentage presumption: (i) Charisma participated in the child's conception with the understanding that she would be a parent; (ii) after the child's birth, Charisma voluntarily assumed parental responsibilities for the three months the three lived together; and (iii) no one else claimed to be the child's second parent.[153] By order dated May 8, 2008, the trial court issued an order concerning child custody and visitation. In that order, the judge granted Kristina sole legal and physical custody of her daughter, who was then five years old, and ordered the parties to meet with a court-appointed psychologist to begin the reunification process between Charisma and Kristina's daughter.[154]

Kristina, a Texas resident since early summer 2005,[155] faces the question of whether Texas courts, despite a state defense of marriage act and constitutional amendment,[156] will permit Charisma to register and enforce the California custody order in the state of Texas. If it does, Kristina could be forced to give visitation to Charisma, a woman with no biological or adoptive relationship with the child.

Other courts have adopted different tests to accomplish the same result. Some courts declare the former partner to be a de facto parent to the child, using a multi-part test to decide whether the legal stranger should be declared a parent over the objections of the child's fit parent. Thus, under that test, some courts require the third party to prove:

"(1) That the biological or adoptive parent consented to, and fostered, the petitioner's formation and establishment of a parent-like relationship with the child; (2) that the petitioner and the child lived together in the same household; (3) that the petitioner assumed obligations of parenthood by taking significant responsibility for the child's care, education and development, including contributing towards the child's support, without expectation of financial compensation; and (4) that the petitioner has been in a parental role for a length of time sufficient to have established with the child a bonded, dependent relationship parental in nature."[157]

The judge in Lisa's case didn't use this test but, in what is probably one of the most egregious examples of judicial activism, plainly created new law from the bench. Judge Cohen in the Rutland Family Court explained that Vermont had not previously "been presented with the question of parental status concerning a child born during a marriage and conceived through artificial insemination." He then created a new test for Vermont to answer the question the legislature hadn't yet answered: "where a legally connected couple utilizes artificial insemination to have a family, parental rights and obligations are determined by facts showing intent to bring a child into the world and raise the child as one's own as part of a family unit, not by biology."[158] In other words, where a woman uses artificial insemination to become pregnant while in a legal union with another woman, the other woman automatically becomes a second mother to the child as long as that woman intended to raise the child as her own. Nothing more is required — she doesn't have to live with the child for any minimum period of time. In fact, under that test, the relationship could end before the child is born and the other woman could still be declared a second mom to the child. Once that happens, according to Vermont courts, the two women are both parents with co-equal constitutional rights.

Other courts have reached similar results simply by using the overarching best interest standard to declare that a child can have three parents: biological mom, biological dad, and mom's former same-sex partner.[159] The possibilities are endless when you are ideologically driven and recognize no restraints on your power. That is why courts in approximately sixteen states have declared legal strangers to be parents over the objections of the child's fit parent. Thankfully, courts in approximately thirteen states have expressly refused to do so.[160]

One example of where this new view of parentage can take us is the story of Joe Price. For several years, Mr. Price was Janet Jenkins' attorney in Virginia as she attempted to have Virginia recognize the Vermont orders. Just a few months before Joe Price first appeared in Virginia courts on behalf of Janet Jenkins, he was featured in a USA Today story in March 2004. The title of the story was "Looking Straight at Gay Parents." The article explained that Joe Price and his partner Victor Zaborsky are the biological fathers to Kim Mosheno's two children. At the time of the article, Ms. Mosheno had a three year old child that was Mr. Price's biological child and was then pregnant with Mr. Zaborsky's biological child. Ms. Mosheno's same-sex partner had already adopted Ms. Mosheno's first child and expected to adopt the second. All four acted as parents to the first child and expected to co-parent the second child as well. Mr. Zaborsky is quoted in the article as admitting that they were "forging new territory"[161] in having the four co-parent the two children. Mr. Price also sought to forge new territory in seeking a court order directing Virginia to give full faith and credit to the Vermont orders. He later had to withdraw as Ms. Jenkins' counsel to focus his attentions in a case where he and his two same-sex partners (who were also his roommates) were charged with obstructing justice, tampering with evidence, and conspiracy, in a case where police state that a male friend of Mr. Price's was sexually assaulted and murdered in Mr. Price's home.[162]

As with the parentage cases, the various court decisions concerning whether marriage laws are constitutional also boil down to whether the courts do their job or overstep their authority and act as legislators. The question in the marriage litigation cases is whether the state has a sufficient interest in continuing to define marriage as the union of one man and one woman. What is a sufficient interest turns on whether sexual orientation is treated by the court as a "suspect classification," such as race. As a result of the 1964 Civil Rights Act, classifications based on race are subject to exacting scrutiny (called "strict scrutiny"), which means that the law classifying based on race will be unconstitutional unless the government can show that it has a compelling justification for the law and that the means used by the law to achieve that compelling justification are the most narrow ones possible. In other words, the law can't discriminate based on race any more than is absolutely necessary.

Pretty much every law discriminating based on race fails because there is no compelling reason to do so. Under federal law, only race and national origin fall into the suspect classification category. Gender falls into intermediate scrutiny, which means the law is unconstitutional unless the government demonstrates that it has an important governmental interest and the means used to achieve that interest are substantially related to the asserted government interest. All other laws that discriminate against a group of people are subject to the rational basis test: the law will be upheld unless the person challenging it demonstrates that the legislature has no legitimate basis for passing the law. In the marriage litigation, those seeking to have the marriage laws declared unconstitutional ask the court to treat sexual orientation as a suspect classification. They know that if a court were to afford suspect classification to sexual orientation, the court would likely declare any challenged law as unconstitutional. That is exactly what happened in the "Prop. 8 Litigation."

The "Prop. 8 Litigation," as it is called, refers to a lawsuit brought in federal court to challenge California's decision to amend its constitution to define marriage as the union of a man and a woman. California voters passed the amendment in November 2008 after the California Supreme Court, in May 2008, declared unconstitutional a previously passed state law with the identical language. The federal lawsuit is but the latest volley in a long-fought battle to protect traditional marriage in California. In 1999, California created a domestic partner registry that permitted same-sex couples to obtain legal recognition for their relationship. In 2000, California voters passed a ballot initiative defining marriage as the union of a man and a woman. Over the next few years, the California legislature passed several bills that eventually gave registered domestic partners all the benefits that previously had only been available for married couples. In February 2004, under the leadership of Mayor Gavin Newsom, San Francisco ignored California law and began marrying same-sex couples, keeping City Hall open over the weekend in order to allow more couples to "marry" before anyone could get to court to attempt to stop the illegal activity. Eventually, the state trial court found that sexual orientation was a suspect classification and declared the marriage laws unconstitutional. After the California Supreme Court affirmed that decision in May 2008, the California voters essentially overturned that decision by writing into the California constitution that marriage is the union of a man and a woman. With no other recourse, homosexual activists turned to federal court, arguing that marriage as the union of one man and one woman violates the federal constitutional guarantees of equal protection and due process.

In what many have criticized as a mockery of justice, Judge Vaughn Walker did what all other federal courts had previously refused to do — he declared sexual orientation to be a suspect class. In his decision, he found that children do not need a mom and a dad to be well-adjusted and that religious beliefs, rather than the homosexual lifestyle, are what harms gays and lesbians. Perhaps not surprisingly, after he issued his "landmark" decision, it became publicly known that he identified as a homosexual, was retiring from the bench, and planned to teach a course at U.C. Berkeley Law School (which isn't exactly known for its conservative bent). As mentioned earlier, a key component in the strategy to gain the "right" to same-sex "marriage," was finding a judge to declare sexual orientation to be a suspect class.

My gut reaction to the question of redefining marriage is that when suspect classification has up to this point been given to immutable characteristics like race and national origin, why should a classification that defines people based on their sexual activity ever be considered for such classification. There are, of course, more reasoned legal explanations why sexual orientation should not be treated as a suspect, or even intermediate, classification.

People undeniably do not choose their race or national origin. Yet, all the evidence thus far demonstrates that there is, at a minimum, some element of choice related to same-sex attractions. In particular, people have to choose to act on those feelings. In addition, none of the categories that receive strict or intermediate scrutiny is based on a person's conduct. Sexual orientation protection would be based on a person's sexual conduct. Some will immediately respond by saying that religion is afforded special constitutional protections (in some circumstances) even though people can choose to change their religious beliefs. One significant difference between religion as a protected status and sexual orientation, however, is that religion is expressly protected in the First Amendment to the Constitution.

Because of the reasons that other categories have been afforded suspect classification, most courts have refused to afford sexual orientation suspect class status; instead they have held that any claims based on sexual orientation discrimination will fail unless the plaintiff can show there's no legitimate government interest in the statute. In the case of the marriage litigation, the plaintiffs need to show that there is no legitimate reason to continue to define marriage as between one man and one woman. Knowing this is a very difficult burden, the plaintiffs often resort to the "animus" argument. Essentially, they argue that the law is based on hatred and moral disapproval alone and, therefore, is illegitimate. In the marriage context, it's hard to prove that the definition of marriage that originated in the Garden of Eden is based solely on hatred and moral disapproval of same-sex couples, yet that is what they are trying to do.

The impact of the efforts to gain rights based on one's sexual orientation do not begin and end in our family courts. Rather, the impact is felt by businesses, doctors, social service agencies, schools, individual citizens, and churches. Let's take a look at a few examples to give you a glimpse of what is taking place.[163]

- A fifty-seven year old man sued a Catholic run hospital in California when the surgical coordinator explained to him that the hospital refused to perform breast augmentation on a male to female transgendered person as part of the sex reassignment process. His lawyers stated it was unlawful for the hospital to rely on its religious beliefs to discriminate against him. The theory behind the case was that because the hospital permits breast augmentation surgeries (e.g., on women after breast cancer) then it is discriminatory to refuse to perform the surgery on a man who has undergone hormone therapy and surgery to attempt to change his gender to a female.[164]

- A medical practice in California was sued when one of the doctors refused to artificially inseminate a woman who desired to have a baby with her same-sex partner. The court explained that the burden on the doctor's religious beliefs is insufficient to allow her to engage in discrimination based on sexual orientation.[165]

- As a result of the Massachusetts court decision redefining marriage as the union of one man and one woman, after more than 100 years of placing children in adopted homes, Catholic Charities of Boston was forced to choose between placing children in the homes of same-sex couples in violation of its religious beliefs or no longer placing children up for adoption. It chose to stop placing children in adoptive homes.[166]

- A Christian photographer in New Mexico was brought before a human rights commission for refusing, on religious grounds, to photograph a same-sex commitment ceremony.[167]

- An Iowa YMCA (Young Men's Christian Association) faced losing a $102,000 grant because it had refused to treat same-sex couples the same as opposite-sex married couples for purposes of the family membership fee.[168]

- A Lutheran high school was sued for expelling two girls who engaged in homosexual conduct. Although the school prohibits all sexual immorality, the fact that the two girls were engaged in same-sex conduct made the school an easy target for a claim of discrimination based on sexual orientation.[169]

- PFOX (Parents and Friends of Ex-Gays and Gays) faces allegations in a Maryland school district that a flyer telling students that change is possible with respect to same-sex attractions constitutes hate speech.[170]

- The Oakland, California city government declared it a hate crime when female city employees organized a Good News Employee Association and announced the group with a flyer that contained the following language: "Marriage is the foundation of the natural family and sustains family values."[171]

- In Canada, we've seen (i) pastors fined and ordered to cease proclaiming the truth of scripture concerning homosexuality, (ii) a university professor fined for expressing his belief to a student that homosexuality is unnatural, and (iii) a city public official fined for stating that homosexuality was not natural.[172]

As people concerned about preserving our freedoms, we need to realize that at the same time that a spiritual battle is taking place for the hearts and souls of those struggling with same-sex attractions, there is a real battle taking place to silence any who disagree with the homosexual agenda.

When I first completed the manuscript for this book, this chapter addressed only the efforts in the counseling profession and courts. Since then, the efforts by our President and Congress to rapidly advance the homosexual agenda requires discussion of those efforts. President Obama has been quite vocal about his views on same-sex relationships and of those who believe that government should not be legally condoning a sinful and personally destructive way of life. In an October 10, 2009 speech before the Human Rights Campaign, he referred to those who believe that marriage is the union of one man and one woman as holding fast "to outworn arguments and old attitudes...."[173] He told the audience that "[y]ou will see a time in which we as a nation finally recognize relationships between two men and two women as just as real and *admirable* as relationships between a man and a woman."[174] The following year, in his Mother's Day and Father's Day proclamations, he echoed his position that same-sex relations are as *admirable* as a married male-female relationship when he stated that "[n]urturing families come in many forms, and children may be raised by" either "two mothers" or "two fathers."[175]

What makes his Mother's Day proclamation statement that nurturing families come in many forms, including two mothers, absurd is that one month later in his Father's Day proclamation he stated the well-known fact that "[a]n active, committed father makes a lasting difference in the life of a child. When fathers are not present, their children and families cope with an absence the government cannot fill." By definition, a two mother household fails to provide the important father figure in a child's life. The commitment of President Obama, and others, to the "politically correct" position that a family with two mothers or two fathers is just as "admirable" as a family headed by a married mother and father, despite the long-lasting negative consequences of the homosexual lifestyle, is disturbing. Nevertheless, consistent with that position, President Obama, and many of his fellow Democrats in Congress, have committed to a repeal of the federal Defense of Marriage Act and to expanding federal laws to include sexual orientation as a protected class, alongside race, religion, age, and gender.

On December 22, 2010, the President signed a law repealing Don't Ask-Don't Tell, which means that men and women who identify as homosexual can openly serve in the military. Shortly after signing the law, a reporter asked President Obama the following question: "is it intellectually consistent to say that gay and lesbians should be able to fight and die for this country but they should not be able to marry the people they love?" The President explained that his "feelings about this are constantly evolving," "that [his] baseline is a strong civil union that provides them the protections and the legal rights that married couples have," and that he will continue to "debate" and "wrestle" with the issue going forward. In other words, he doesn't rule out the possibility that he would support same-sex "marriage."

On February 23, 2011, the President also instructed the United States Department of Justice to no longer defend Section 3 of the federal Defense of Marriage Act (DOMA) in litigation pending throughout the nation. In a six-page letter addressed to Speaker of the House John Boehner, Attorney

General Eric Holder stated that he and the President had concluded that the federal law defining marriage as the union of one man and one woman, for purposes of interpreting and applying all federal laws and regulations, was unconstitutional. Not only does the President's decision directly conflict with prior case precedent, it also directly ignores the separation of powers built into our frame of government: the Constitution does not contain any right to same-sex marriage; the President's decision to the contrary is a classic case of the executive branch exceeding its constitutional authority by attempting to "make law," which is unquestionably a power delegated to the legislature — not the courts or the executive.

In taking these various steps to support civil unions and same-sex marriage, the President, his administration, and the Democratic party have openly taken the position that America should put its stamp of approval on conduct the Bible calls sinful. At the same time, they seek to silence and minimize those who stand on Biblical principles. We need to realize that the battle lines have been drawn; we are at war.

I believe Chai Feldblum got it right when she characterized the battle as a "zero-sum game." We need to realize that it is a zero sum game — there will be a winner and a loser in this battle and the outcome will affect us all. The question now is what can we do to win this battle. The most important first step is to get off the sidelines and into the battle before we are silenced.

During the course of Lisa's nearly seven year legal battle, the attorneys for Janet Jenkins tried various tactics to silence Lisa by preventing her attorneys from representing Lisa in court. One of the latest tactics occurred in June 2010 as I prepared to argue before the Vermont Supreme Court on Lisa's behalf. Because I am not admitted to practice in Vermont, I had to ask permission to represent Lisa at oral argument. Janet's attorneys opposed my motion, arguing that I had shown disrespect for the authority of the Vermont Supreme Court. Just what did I say that caused Janet's attorneys to suggest that I was not fit to argue before the court? According to the papers submitted on June 7, 2010, I had shown disrespect because of my (i) assertion that "No court (or legislature, or executive) in the United States has the authority to strip a fit, biological parent of her fundamental rights without affording her the constitutionally required due process" and (ii) reliance on the Declaration of Independence to remind the court that after a long train of abuses against our inalienable rights, "there comes a time when government abuses require the people to throw off abusive government...." In other words, my reminding the court that it does not have unlimited power but instead has the duty to protect citizens' unalienable rights caused Janet's attorneys to argue that I was not fit to argue on Lisa's behalf.

Not surprisingly, the Vermont Supreme Court eventually upheld the trial court's decision to strip Lisa of custody of her child and the U.S. Supreme Court refused to hear Lisa's appeal of the Virginia order. In December 2010, Lisa's seven year legal battle came to an end. At this point, although no one seems to know Lisa's whereabouts, Virginia and Vermont courts stand ready to take Isabella from Lisa and turn Isabella over to Janet — not because Lisa is anything other than a fit parent, but because Lisa refused to comply with court orders that would have exposed Isabella to the homosexual lifestyle.

In September 2008, frustrated with what she saw as apathy among many Christians to the abuses taking place, Lisa wrote:

> "Too many people are apathetic, asking themselves 'what can I do,' offering excuses such as 'I am only one person, I don't have time, I can't take a stand now,' or telling themselves and others that the whole thing is 'in God's hands.' Although God is definitely in control of our lives, we are called to act. We are the disciples for this moment; we are to go and do. We are to go and gather others as the disciples did in order to do God's work. I believe we are called to tell the people of this Nation about the activist judges and warn them about the threats to our freedoms.... I am at a loss of words on why people are choosing to remain silent. All I know is that one day I am going to see Jesus and He is going to ask me what I did for Him. I want to tell Him that I did my best and that I exhausted all my resources for Him."

A Few Parting Thoughts

When I think about what I've discussed in this book, many things grieve my heart. My heart grieves over the fact that we live in a culture that intentionally seeks to rob people of living the life their Creator intended for them. We tell people that they are born gay, can't change, and this is the best it will ever be. We encourage them to stay in relationships that are personally, physically, and mentally harmful. We intentionally create a society where we encourage people to pursue a path of self-destruction rather than true fulfillment and happiness.

My heart also grieves over the failure of the Church to be Christ to those struggling with same-sex attractions. We are called to bring love and truth to all, yet for so long we have brought only condemnation or alienation to those with same-sex attractions. We need to step up to the plate and be available to be used by God to minister to those struggling with same-sex attractions.

And my heart grieves over the apathy and blindness in our society to the significant threat to our religious and free speech liberties as a result of the relentless, longsuffering pursuit of rights based on "sexual orientation." We cannot afford to bury our heads in the sand and pretend the danger doesn't exist, that someone else will fight the battle, or that it doesn't affect us.

We are commanded to be salt and light to the world: to be light to those struggling with same-sex attractions while at the same time salt in the culture to stand for what is right. If we do nothing, and lose this war, we will be silenced. If we win, however, we preserve the rights to free speech and religious liberties so we can continue to spread a message of hope and healing to hurting people.

Please pray how God can use you to be light to those who need Christ and salt to a culture that needs more than ever to hear the truth of the Gospel.

Endnotes

1 The Appendix contains several helpful books to understand the influence of childhood experiences on developing same-sex attractions.

2 For a more thorough discussion of the issues discussed in this chapter, offered by those who counsel men and women struggling with same-sex attractions, see Bob Davies & Lori Rentzel, *Coming Out of Homosexuality: New Freedom for Men & Women* (InterVarsity Press 1993). This book was instrumental in helping Lisa begin to determine the triggers in her life that caused her to be attracted to women.

3 Richard Luscombe, *US Girls Embrace Gay Passion Fashion, The Observer*, Jan. 4, 2004, available at http://www.guardian.co.uk/world/2004/jan/04/usa.gayrights.

4 *See, e.g.,* Gary J. Gates, *Geographic Trends Among Same-Sex Couples in the U.S. Census and The American Community Survey* at 8 (Nov. 2007) (stating that based on the National Survey of Family Growth, which is published by the US Centers for Disease Control and Prevention, approximately 4.1% of men and women aged 18-44 identify themselves as gay or lesbian).

5 *See, e.g.,* Walter Schumm, *Children of Homosexuals more apt to be homosexuals? A reply to Morrison and to Cameron based on an examination of multiple sources of data*, J. Biosoc. Sci. 2010 Nov; 42(6): 721-42.

6 *See, e.g., Life Coaches for Kids*, available at http://www.lifecoaches.org/Web/Research.asp (citing studies finding that 72% of adolescent murderers grew up without fathers, 70% of juveniles in state-operated reform institutions grew up without fathers, and 85% of all youth in prison came from fatherless homes).

7 *Baker v. General Motors Corp.*, 522 U.S. 222, 233, 235 (1998) (emphasis added); *see also Olmsted v. Olmsted*, 216 U.S. 386, 394 (1910) (while judgment is "conclusive on the merits," it can only be "executed in the latter [state] as its laws permit"); *Fall v. Estin*, 215 U.S. 1 (1909); *Johnson v. Johnson*, 849 N.E.2d

1176, 1179-80 (Ind. Ct. App. 2006); Charles Alan Wright, et al., Federal Practice and Procedure § 4467 (discussing the distinction between enforcement and recognition for purposes of a money judgment).

8   An April 13, 2011 decision by the Fifth Circuit Court of Appeals relied on this enforcement distinction to conclude that a same-sex couple from New York who had adopted in New York a Louisiana-born child could not require Louisiana to enforce the adoption by changing the birth certificate to reflect that the child had two fathers. *Adar v. Smith*, No. 09-30036 (5th Cir. Apr. 13, 2011) (*en banc*).

9   *Hood v. McGhee*, 237 U.S. 611 (1915).

10   *See Thompson v. Thompson*, 484 U.S. 174, 183 (1988).

11   *Id*. at 177 (quoting Pub. L. 96-611, 94 Stat. 3569 §7(c)(5).

12   *See* 28 U.S.C. 1738A.

13   *Thompson*, 484 U.S. at 183.

14   484 U.S. at 183 (emphasis added).

15   *See* S. Rep. 103-361, at 4, 1994 U.S.C.C.A.N. 3259, 3261; *Ex Parte N.B.*, No. 1080440, ___ So. 3d ___ , 2010 WL 2629064, at *5 (Ala. June 30, 2010) ("questions regarding the judgment of the California trial court and its enforceability in Alabama may exist in light of the unequivocal nature of Alabama public policy on the issue presented by this case"); *Mason v Mason*, 775 N.E.2d 706, 709 & n.3 (Ind. Ct. App. 2002) (stating the general rule that courts will give full faith and credit to marriage validly contracted in the place where it is celebrated, unless it violates strong public policy); Ala. Op. Att'y Gen. No. 2000-129, 2000 WL 33310632, at *7 (Apr. 20, 2000) ("the Full Faith and Credit Clause would not require the State of Alabama ... to recognize any form of homosexual 'marriage' that might be conducted in the future under the laws of the state of Vermont, whether the relationship were legally styled a 'marriage,' a 'civil union,' or a 'domestic partnership.'").

16   28 U.S.C. § 1738C; H.R. Rep. 104-664, at 27, 1996 U.S.C.C.A.N. 2905, 2932.

17   H.R. Rep. 104-664 at 24, 1996 U.S.C.C.A.N at 2929.

18   *Id*. at n.21 (emphasis added) (citations omitted).

19 *See Elk Grove Unified Sch. Dist v. Newdow*, 542 U.S. 1, 12 (2004).

20 *The Federalist*, No. 45, at 289 (Clinton Rossiter, ed. 1961).

21 *Id.*

22 *Rose v. Rose*, 481 U.S. 619, 625 (1987).

23 *Cf.* Ala. Atty Gen'l Op. No. 2000-129, 2000 WL 33310632 (Apr. 20, 2000); *Nat'l Pride at Work v. Mich.*, 732 N.W.2d 139, 150 (Mich. Ct. App. 2007) (public employers' recognition of domestic partnership agreements for purposes of establishing eligibility for employment benefits violated marriage amendment, which prohibited recognition of same-sex marriage or "similar union"), *aff'd*, 748 N.W.2d 524 (Mich. 2008).

24 The Supreme Court precedent refers to the parent-child relationship in the context of "blood relationships," a parents' interest in their "natural" children, and father's interest in the children he has "sired." *See, e.g., Santosky v. Kramer*, 455 U.S. 745, 753 (1982); *Stanley v. Illinois*, 405 U.S. 645, 651 (1972).

25 *Ephesians* 6:4.

26 *Id.*

27 *Troxel v. Granville*, 530 U.S. 57, 65 (2000).

28 *Pierce v. Soc'y of Sisters*, 268 U.S. 510, 535 (1925).

29 *Prince v. Massachusetts*, 321 U.S. 158, 166 (1944) (citing *Pierce*, 268 U.S. at 535).

30 *Troxel v. Granville*, 530 U.S. 57 (2000).

31 For similar reasons, I believe it violates a fit parent's rights to order visitation in favor of any third party, including grandparents, over the parent's objections.

32 *Rogers v. Tennessee*, 532 U.S. 451, 460 (2001).

33 *See* 1 V.S.A. § 213 ("Act of the general assembly ... shall not affect a suit begun or pending at the time of their passage"); *Potomac Hosp. Corp. v Dillon*, 229 Va. 355, 358-59, 329 S.E.2d 41, 44 (Va. 1985) (substantive and vested rights are included within those interests protected from retroactive application of statutes").

34 See, e.g., State v. Jess, 184 P.3d 133 (Haw. 2008) (subjecting new court-created procedural rule to same constitutional due process inquiry as legislative enactments).

35 See Stadter v. Siperko, 661 S.E.2d 494 (Va. Ct. App. 2008).

36 Id. at 498 (quoting Bailes v. Sours, 340 S.E.2d 824, 827 (Va. 1986)).

37 Goodridge v. Dep't of Health, 798 N.E.2d 491 (Mass. 2003).

38 See, e.g., Standhardt v. Superior Court, 77 P.3d 451 (Ariz. Ct. App. 2003) (marriage laws constitutional); In re Marriage Cases, 183 P.3d 384 (Cal. 2008) (marriage laws unconstitutional); Kerrigan v. Dep't of Public Health, 957 A.2d 407 (Conn. 2008) (civil union statute unconstitutional); O'Kelley v. Perdue, 632 S.E.2d 110 (Ga. 2006) (marriage laws constitutional); Morrison v. Sadler, 821 N.E.2d 15 (Ind. Ct. App. 2005) (constitutional); Conaway v. Deane, 932 A.2d 571 (Md. 2007) (marriage laws constitutional); Lewis v. Harris, 908 A.2d 196 (N.J. 2006) (marriage laws unconstitutional); Hernandez v. Robles, 7 N.Y.3d 338 (N.Y. 2006) (constitutional); Andersen v. King Co., 138 P.3d 963 (Wash. 2006) (marriage laws constitutional); see also Wilson v. Ake, 354 F. Supp. 2d 1298 (M.D. Fla. 2005) (upholding constitutionality of DOMA).

39 See, e.g., Lofton v. Sec'y of Dep't of Children and Family Servs., 353 F.3d 801 (11th Cir. 2004) (upholding Florida's ban on homosexual adoption); see also Finstuen v. Crutcher, 496 F.3d 1139 (10th Cir. 2007) (declaring unconstitutional an Oklahoma statute that denied recognition of same adoptions).

40 See Rena M. Lindevaldsen, Sacrificing Motherhood on the Altar of Political Correctness: Declaring a Legal Stranger to Be a Parent Over the Objections of the Child's Biological Parent, 21 Regent U. L. Rev. 1, 16 & nn.107-108 (listing cases decided in more than twenty five states involving claims to visitation, custody, or parentage rights on behalf of third parties).

41 Printz v. U.S., 521 U.S. 898, 921-22 (1997) (citations omitted); see also U.S. v. Lopez, 514 U.S. 549, 552 (1995) ("This constitutionally mandated division of authority 'was adopted by the Framers to ensure protection of our fundamental liberties.' 'Just as the separation and independence of the coordinate branches of the Federal Government serve to prevent the accumulation of excessive power in any one branch, a healthy balance of power between the

States and the Federal Government will reduce the risk of tyranny and abuse from either front."') (citations omitted).

42 FEDERALIST No. 45 at 289 (James Madison) (Signet Classic 2003).

43 *Ankenbrandt v. Richards*, 504 U.S. 689, 692 (1992).

44 Maggie Gallagher, *the Abolition of Marriage* 113-14 (Regnery Publishing 1996).

45 According to a 2005 CDC Report, those identifying as "homosexual" or "bisexual" report nearly double the rates of sexually transmitted infections among 15-44 year olds. William D. Mosher, et al., *Sexual Behavior and Selected Health Measures: Men and Women 15-44 Years of Age, United States, 2002*, at 37 (U.S. Department of Health and Human Services Advance Data from Vital and Health Statistics September 15, 2005), available at http://www.cdc.gov/STD/SEE/MSM/SEE-MSM-HCP.pdf; *see also A Guide for Health Care Professionals: Screening and Testing Men Who Have Sex With Men (MSM) for Syphilis*, at 1 ("nearly all counties with a high incidence of syphilis cases ... are in the South or in large metropolitan areas with sizable men who have sex with men (MSM) populations").

46 Pastor Daniel Henderson, Thomas Road Baptist Church, January 17, 2010.

47 Alan Chambers, *God's Grace and the Homosexual Next Door* 123-24 (Harvest House Publishing 2006).

48 *Id.* at 122.

49 For a great book on the issue of holiness for our lives, see Jerry Bridges, *The Pursuit of Holiness* 22 (NavPress 2006).

50 II *Timothy* 2:22.

51 Bob Davies & Lori Rentzel, *Coming Out of Homosexuality: New Freedom for Men & Women* (Harvest House Publishers 1993).

52 Patricia Nell Warren, "Future Shock", *The Advocate*, October 3, 1995.

53 For a more thorough discussion of the religious liberties implications of the growing movement to normalize homosexual behavior *see* Rena M. Lindevaldsen, *The Fallacy of Neutrality from Beginning to End: The Battle Between Reli-*

gious Liberties and Rights Based on Homosexual Conduct, 4 Liberty U. L. Rev. 425 (Spring 2010).

54   Andrea Peyser, "La Cage a Folly in School," *New York Post* (June 17, 2010), available at http://www.nypost.com/p/news/national/la_cage_folly_in_school_vpvD8liqeJlskghtU9VORO.

55   School Field Trip to Teacher's Lesbian Wedding Sparks Controversy (Oct. 13, 2008), http://www.foxnews.com/story/0,2933,436961,00.html.

56   San Francisco Unified School District LGBTQ Support Services, www.healthiersf.org/LGBTQ/InTheClassroom/voices-susan.html.

57   Abigail Curtis, *State Rules in Favor of Young Transgender*, *Bangor Daily News*, July 1, 2009, http://www.bangordailynews.com/detail/109732.html.

58   *See, e.g.*, Mark Tapscott, *Obama Appointee Lauded NAMBLA Figure*, THE EXAMINER, Oct. 1, 2009, http://www.washingtonexaminer.com/opinion/blogs/beltway-confidential/Obama-appointee-lauded-NAMBLA-figure-63115112.html.

59   Maxim Lott, *Critics Assail Obama's "Safe School" Czar, Say He's Wrong Man for the Job*, Sept. 23, 2009, http://www.foxnews.com/politics/2009/09/23/critics-assail-obamas-safe-schools-czar-say-hes-wrong-man-job/.

60   Former Student Defends Obama's "Safe Schools" Czar Against Allegations (Oct. 3, 2009), http://www.foxnews.com/politics/2009/10/03/student-defends-obamas-safe-schools-czar-allegations/.

61   *See* GLSEN, What We Do page, http://www.glsen.org/cgi-bin/iowa/all/what/index.html (providing links to Day of Silence, No Name Calling Week, and Gay Straight Alliances); GLSEN, Ally Week, http://www.allyweek.org/; GLSEN, *Students Celebrate GLSEN's TransAction! To Educate Peers About Gender* (Feb. 27, 2009), http://glsen.org/cgi-bin/iowa/all/news/record/2383.html.

62   GLSEN, FROM DENIAL TO DENIGRATION: UNDERSTANDING INSTITUTIONALIZED HETEROSEXISM IN OUR SCHOOLS (2002), http://www.glsen.org/binary-data/GLSEN_ATTACHMENTS/file/222-1.pdf.

63   *Id.* at 1.

64   *Id.*

65 *See* Ally Week, About Ally Week (FAQs) page, http://www.allyweek.com/about/index.cfm.

66 *See* Ally Week, Student and Educators page, available at http://www.allyweek.com/studentseducators/index.cfm.

67 *See* Day of Silence website at http://www.dayofsilence.org/index.cfm.

68 Gay Straight Alliance Network et al, "Beyond the Binary" (2004), http://www.transgenderlawcenter.org/pdf/beyond_the_binary.pdf (last visited Dec. 3, 2010); Lambda Legal et al., "Bending the Mold: An Action Kit for Transgender Students" (2007), http:www.nyacyouth.org/docs/uploads/LL_TransKit_FINAL_Lores.pdf (last visited Dec. 3, 2010).

69 GLSEN, "Gender Terminology."

70 *See* PFLAG website, http://community.pflag.org/Page.aspx?pid=194&srcid=-2; *see also* PFLAG, *Be Yourself: Questions and Answers for Gay, Lesbian, Bisexual, and Transgendered Youth*, http://www.pflag.org/fileadmin/user_upload/Publications/Be_Yourself.pdf.

71 *Be Yourself* at 3-4, http://www.pflag.org/fileadmin/user_upload/Publications/Be_Yourself.pdf.

72 *Id.* at 4.

73 *Id.* at 7.

74 Batavia High School, Gender Identity Awareness: Presentation for Batavia High School Students (on file with the author).

75 *Id.*

76 *Id.*

77 According to a July 1, 2009 State Policies in Brief from the Guttmacher Institute, twenty-one states and the District of Columbia mandate that schools teach sex education (Delaware, District of Columbia, Florida, Georgia, Hawaii, Iowa, Kansas, Kentucky, Maine, Maryland, Minnesota, Montana, Nevada, New Jersey, New Mexico, North Carolina, Oregon, Rhode Island, South Carolina, Tennessee, Utah, Vermont, and West Virginia.), and thirty-five states and the District of Columbia mandate STD/HIV education (Alabama, California, Connecticut, Delaware, District of Columbia, Florida, Georgia, Hawaii,

Indiana, Iowa, Kansas, Kentucky, Maine, Maryland, Michigan, Minnesota, Missouri, Montana, Nevada, New Hampshire, New Jersey, New Mexico, New York, North Carolina, Ohio, Oklahoma, Oregon, Pennsylvania, Rhode Island, South Carolina, Tennessee, Utah, Vermont, Washington, West Virginia, and Wisconsin). *See* Guttmacher Institute, State Policies in Brief: Sex and STI/ HIV Education (July 1, 2009), available at www.guttmacher.org/pubs/spib_ SE.pdf (last visited October 24, 2009). Only two of the thirty-five states that have mandatory sex education or STD/HIV education require prior parental permission (Nevada and Utah). While all but three of the remaining states that have mandatory sex or STD/HIV education permit parents to opt their children out of the curriculum under *some* circumstances (Indiana, Kentucky, and North Carolina do not permit parental opt-out).

78 California, for example, requires schools to send a notice at the beginning of each year in which there is sex or STD/HIV education. The parents must be given the opportunity to review the instructional materials at the school and the opportunity to request in writing that their child not participate in the instruction. The law, however, does not permit students to opt out of anti-harassment programs or other instruction that discusses gender, sexual orientation, or family life that does not discuss human reproductive organs and their functions. *See* Cal. Educ. Code § 51938.

79 *Troxel v. Granville*, 530 U.S. 57, 65 (2000).

80 *Pierce v. Society of Sisters*, 268 U.S. 510, 535 (1925).

81 *Prince v. Commonwealth of Mass.*, 321 U.S. 158, 166 (1944).

82 *See Santosky II v. Kramer*, 455 U.S. 745, 766-67 (1982) (a "clear and convincing evidence" standard of proof is the minimal standard of proof required to satisfy due process in a termination of parental rights hearing); *Garcia v. Rubio*, 670 N.W.2d 475, 483 (Neb. Ct. App. 2003) ("A court may not, in derogation of the superior right of a biological or adoptive parent, grant child custody to one who is not a biological or adoptive parent unless the biological or adoptive parent is unfit to have the child custody or has legally lost the parental superior right in a child.").

83 *Stanley v. Illinois*, 405 U.S. 645, 651 (1972) (dealing with rights of an unwed father).

84 *M.L.B. v. S.L.J.*, 519 U.S. 102, 116 (1996) (citations omitted).

85 *Stanley*, 405 U.S. at 657-58.

86 *Bethel Sch. Dist. No. 403 v. Fraser*, 478 U.S. 675, 683 (1986).

87 *Sheff v. O'Neill*, 678 A.2d 1267, 1289-90 (Conn. 1996) (quoting *Brown v. Board of Educ.*, 347 U.S. 483, 493 (1954) and *Plyler v. Doe*, 457 U.S. 202, 221 (1982)).

88 *Parents United for Better Schools, Inc. v. Sch. Dist. of Philadelphia Bd. of Educ.*, 148 F.3d 260, 271 (3d Cir. 1998).

89 *Roman v. Appleby*, 558 F. Supp. 449, 456 (C.D. Penn. 1983) (citations to other cases omitted).

90 *Id.*

91 *Id.*

92 68 F.3d 525 (1st Cir. 1995).

93 *Id.* at 529.

94 *Id.* at 533.

95 *Id.* at 533-34.

96 *Curtis v. School Committee of Falmouth*, 652 N.E.2d 580 (Mass. 1995).

97 *Id.* at 757-58.

98 *Fields v. Palmdale Sch. Dist.*, 427 F.3d 1197 (9th Cir. 2005), opinion amended on denial of reh'g, 447 F.3d 1187 (9th Cir. 2006).

99 427 F.3d at 1202, n.3.

100 *Id.* at 1206 (quoting a *Blau v. Fort Thomas Pub. Sch. Dist.*, 401 F.3d 381, 395-96 (6th Cir. 2005)).

101 *Johnson v. Dade Co. Public Schools*, No. 91-2952, 1992 WL 466902 (S.D. Fla. 1992).

102 *Id.* at * 10.

103 *Parker v. Hurley*, 474 F. Supp. 2d 261 (D. Mass. 2007), *aff'd* 514 F.3d 87 (1st Cir. 2008).

104   *Id.* at 263-64.

105   *Id.* at 265.

106   *Id.* at 271.

107   *Id.* at 274.

108   *Id.* at 275.

109   Report of the American Psychological Association Task Force on Appropriate Therapeutic Response to Sexual Orientation at 2 (Aug. 2009) (hereinafter "Task Force Report").

110   *Id.* at 2; see Mathew D. Staver, *Same-Sex Marriage: Putting Every Household at Risk* 10-11 (2004) (quoting homosexual activist and writer Michelangelo Signorile).

111   Task Force Report at 18, 47, 50, 58, 60, 72-73.

112   *Id.* at 76.

113   *Id.* at 6.

114   In the Northwest Ordinance, signed by President Washington in 1789, he stated "Religion, morality, and knowledge, being necessary to good government and the happiness of mankind, schools and the means of education shall forever be encouraged."

115   Benjamin Rush, "Of the Mode of Education Proper in a Republic," 1798.

116   Noah Webster's Advice to the Young (WallBuilder Press 1993).

117   *Plyler v. Doe*, 457 U.S. 202, 221 (1982).

118   Alexis DeTocqueville, *Democracy in America* 342 (Henry Reeve trans., D. Appleton & Co. 1904) (1835).

119   *Bethel Sch. Dist. No. 403 v. Fraser*, 478 U.S. 675, 683 (1986) (emphasis added).

120   GLSEN, *2007 National School Climate Survey: The experiences of lesbian, gay, bisexual and transgender youth in our nation's schools* 100 (2008).

121   *Id.*

122   *Id.*

123 Chai Feldblum, *Moral Conflict and Liberty: Gay Rights and Religion*, 72 Brook.
     L. Rev. 61, 97 (2006).

124 Task Force Report at 11.

125 *See* Joseph Nicolosi, Ph.D., "APA Task Force Report — A Mockery of Science,"
     available at http://www.josephnicolosi.com/apa-task-force/.

126 Task Force Report at 2.

127 Task Force Report at 15-19, 58.

128 Joy Whitman, et al., *Ethical Issues Related to Reparative or Conversion Therapy*,
     May 22, 2006, http://www.counseling.org/PressRoom/NewsReleases.aspx?
     AGuid=b68aba97-2f08-40c2-a400-0630765f72f4.

129 *Id.*

130 American Counseling Association, *State Licensure Boards That Have Adopted
     the ACA Code of Ethics*, 2010, http://www.counseling.org/Counselors/
     LicensureAndCert.aspx (link to chart is available on this page); *see also*
     Truth Wins Out & Lambda Legal, *Pray Away the Gay*, at 10, http://www.
     truthwinsout.org/wp-content/uploads/2009/02/exgay_booklet1.pdf;   *see,
     e.g.*, Adrienne S. Gaines, *Christian Counselor Who Refused to Offer Gay Sex
     Therapy Loses Case*, Charisma News Online, Dec. 2, 2009, available at http://
     www.charismamag.com/index.php/news/25520-christian-counselor-who-
     refused-to-offer-gay-sex-therapy-loses-case.

131 Am. Psychiatric Ass'n, Diagnostic and Statistical Manual of
     Mental Disorders 5352 (4th ed. 1994).

132 *See, e.g., In re Marriage Cases*, 183 P.3d 384, 441 & n.59 (Cal. 2008) (relying
     on APA's definition of "sexual orientation"); *Kerrigan v. Commissioner of Public
     Health*, 957 A.2d 407, 435 (Ct. 2008) (relying on APA literature for the conclu-
     sion that "homosexual orientation 'implies no impairment in judgment, stability,
     reliability or general social or vocational capabilities'" (citation omitted)); *In re
     Adoption of Doe*, 2008 WL 5006172, at *7 (Fla. Cir. Ct. 2008) (relying on APA
     literature concerning stability of same-sex relationships); *Varnum v. Brien*, 763
     N.S.2d 862, 874 (Iowa 2009) (relying on APA literature concerning ability of
     same-sex partners to parent); *Kulstad v. Maniaci*, 2009 MT 326, ⟨⟨ 34, 43,

352 Mont. 513, 220 P.3d 595 (relying on APA literature regarding effects of children raised in same-sex households).

133   *Ward v. Wilbanks*, No. 09-11237, 2010 WL 3026428 (E.D. Mich. July 26, 2010).

134   Blackstone's Commentaries, Section the Second, *Of the Laws of Nature*, at 41.

135   *Charisma R. v. Kristina S.*, 44 Cal. Rptr. 3d 332, 333 (Cal. Ct. App. 2006).

136   *Charisma R.*, 44 Cal. Rptr. 3d at 333. At that time, pursuant to AB 25 and 26, a registered domestic partner was treated as the spouse of a taxpayer for purposes of: (i) several state tax deductions relating to medical care and health care costs; (ii) certain unemployment benefits; (iii) maintaining a cause of action for negligent infliction of emotional distress; (iv) second parent adoption; (v) governmental health care coverage upon death of partner; (vi) health care decisions; (vii) sick leave; (viii) disability benefits; and (ix) certain probate matters. It was not until January 1, 2005, through AB 205, that California afforded domestic partners the same rights and benefits as married couples.

137   *Id.*

138   *Id.*

139   *Id.; see also Sharon S. v. Superior Court*, 73 P.3d 554 (Cal. 2003) (permitting same-sex couples to use the second parent adoption statute).

140   *Id.*

141   A copy is on file with the author.

142   *Id.*

143   *Id.*

144   *Id.; see also* Cal. Fam. Code § 7600 *et seq.* (Uniform Parentage Act).

145   *Id.; see also West v. Superior Ct.*, 69 Cal. Rptr. 2d 160 (Cal. Ct. App. 1997) (former same-sex partner lacked standing as parent under Uniform Parentage Act); *Nancy S. v. Michele G.*, 279 Cal. Rptr. 212 (Cal. Ct. App. 1991) (same); *Curiale v. Reagan*, 272 Cal. Rptr. 520 (Cal. Ct. App. 1990) (same).

146   *Id.*

147 Paternity is defined as "the relation of a father." American Dictionary of the English Language (Noah Webster 1828); *see also* Black's Law Dictionary 1163 (8th ed.) ("The state or condition of being a father"). "Presumption of paternity" and "presumption of maternity" are separately defined, reflecting the inherent differences between a mother and a father. *See, e.g.,* Black's Law Dictionary at 1225.

148 *Elisa B. v. Superior Court,* 117 P.3d 660, 666-67 (Cal. 2005). Prior to the August 2005 decisions, the court had explained that "the 'parent and child relationship' is thus a legal relationship encompassing two kinds of parents, 'natural' and 'adoptive.'" *Johnson v. Calvert,* 851 P.2d 776, 781 (Cal. 1993). In that case, the court refused to declare the surrogate a mother over the objection of the intended parents. *Id.* It was not until August 2003 that the court declared that a mother could consent to a second parent adoption by her same-sex partner. *Sharon S. v. Superior Court,* 73 P.3d 554, 574 (Cal. 2003).

149 *See* Cal. Fam. Code § 7611(d).

150 *Id.* at 671-72.

151 44 Cal. Rptr. 3d at 336. The court explained that presumed parent status depends upon affirmative findings that Charisma received the baby into her home and openly held her out as her natural child. *Id.*

152 *Charisma R. v. Krinsta S.,* no. HF0415383, Order after Hearing, at 2 (Super. Ct. Dec. 27, 2006).

153 *Id.* at 3-4. In *Elisa B.,* the Supreme Court explained its decision to declare that a child could have two mommies by emphasizing the importance of two parents to provide emotional and financial support. 117 P.3d at 669.

154 *Charisma R. v. Kristina S.,* no. HF0415383, Statement of Decision and Ruling on Issues of Child Custody and Visitation, at 14-15 (Super. Ct. May 8, 2008).

155 Kristina became a Texas resident nearly one year *after* the trial court holding that Charisma lacked standing to seek parental rights, two months before the California Supreme Court held for the first time that a child could have two mothers without the use of second parent adoption, and nearly eighteen months before the trial court, on remand, declared Charisma to be a parent to Kristina's child.

156   In its constitution, Texas declares that "[m]arriage ... shall consist only of the union of one man and one woman," and that "[t]his state or a political subdivision of this state may not create or recognize any legal status identical or similar to marriage." TEXAS CONST. art. 1, § 32. By statute, Texas defined "'civil union'" as "any relationship status other than marriage that: (1) is intended as an alternative to marriage or applies primarily to cohabiting persons; and (2) grants to the parties of the relationship legal protections, benefits, or responsibilities granted to the spouses of a marriage." The statute then declares that a "marriage between persons of the same sex or a civil union is contrary to the public policy of this state and is void in this state" and that the "state or an agency or political subdivision of the state may not give effect to a: (1) public act, record, or judicial proceeding that creates, recognizes, or validates a marriage between persons of the same sex or a civil union in this state or in any other jurisdiction; or (2) right or claim to any legal protection, benefit, or responsibility asserted as a result of a marriage between persons of the same sex or a civil union in this state or in any other jurisdiction." Tex. Fam. Code § 6.204.

157   *Holtzman v. Knott*, 533 N.W.2d 419, 421 (Wis. 1995).

158   November 2004 Parentage Order at 11.

159   *See, e.g., Jacob v. Schultz-Jacob*, 923 A.2d 473 (Pa. Super. Ct. 2007); *Carvin v. Britain*, 122 P.3d 161 (Wash. 2005) (*en banc*).

160   *See* Rena M. Lindevaldsen, *Sacrificing Motherhood on the Altar of Political Correctness: Declaring a Legal Stranger to Be a Parent Over the Objections of the Child's Biological Parent*, 21 Regent U. L. Rev. 1, 16 & nn. 106-107 (2008) (listing cases that have treated third parties as parents and those cases that have refused to do so).

161   Karen S. Peterson, *Looking Straight at Gay Parents*, USA *Today*, March 3, 2004, available at http://www.usatoday.com/life/lifestyle/2004-03-09-gay-parents_x.htm.

162   The Affidavit in Support of an Arrest Warrant is available at http://who murderedrobertwone.com/legal-documents/. A *Washington Post* article discussing the case is available at http://www.washingtonpost.com/wp-dyn/content/article/2008/11/20/AR2008112001554.html.

163 These examples and others are discussed in Rena M. Lindevaldsen, *The Fallacy of Neutrality from Beginning to End: The Battle Between Religious Liberties and Rights Based on Homosexual Conduct*, 4 Liberty U. L. Rev. 425 (2010).

164 *Catholic Hospital Sued for Refusing Breast Implants to "Transgendered,"* Jan. 9, 2008, available at http://www.catholicnewsagency.com/news/catholic_hospital_sued_for_refusing_breast_implants_to_transgendered/.

165 *North Coast Women's Care Medical Group, Inc. v. San Diego County Superior Court*, 189 P.3d 959 (Cal. 2008).

166 Patricia Wen, *Catholic Charities Stuns State, Ends Adoptions*, The Boston Globe, March 11, 2006, available at http://www.boston.com/news/local/articles/2006/03/11/catholic_charities_stuns_state_ends_adoptions/.

167 *Willock v. Elane Photography, LLC*, HRD No. 06-12-20-0685 (New Mexico Human Rights Commission April 2008), decision available at http://www.scribd.com/doc/24425459/Elainte-Photography-LLC-v-Vanessa-Willock-N-M-2nd-Dist-2008-06632-Dec-11-2009.

168 *Lesbian Couple Ready to Take Des Moines Y to Court*, available at http://clubindustry.com/news/lesbian-couple-ymca-court/.

169 *Where's the Discrimination?*, California Catholic Daily, Sept. 15, 2007, available at http://www.calcatholic.com/news/newsArticle.aspx?id=f1b804c0-d29f-4f77-90d5-0c2da25b6687.

170 Bob Unruh, *Christian Speech Targeted as Hate*, Feb. 9, 2010, available at http://www.wnd.com/index.php?pageId=124553.

171 George F. Will, *Speech Police, Riding High in Oakland*, The Washington Post, June 24, 2007, available at http://www.washingtonpost.com/wp-dyn/content/article/2007/06/22/AR2007062201704.html.

172 *See* Colleen Raezler, *Will Religious Teaching about Homosexuality be Prosecuted as a Hate Crime?*, Culture and Media Institute, Oct. 28, 2009, available at http://www.cultureandmediainstitute.org/articles/2009/20091028100823.aspx; *Canadian Pastor Fined and Gagged Over Gay Comments*, The Christian Institute, June 10, 2008, available at http://www.christian.org.uk/news/canadian-pastor-fined-and-gagged-over-gay-comments/.

173   Transcript of the speech is available at http://www.whitehouse.gov/the-press-office/remarks-president-human-rights-campaign-dinner.

174   *Id.* (emphasis added).

175   *See* Presidential Proclamation — Mother's Day, available at http://www.white-house.gov/the-press-office/presidential-proclamation-mothers-day, and Presidential Proclamation — Father's Day, available at http://www.whitehouse.gov/the-press-office/presidential-proclamation-fathers-day.

176   Taken from *A Christian Manifesto* by Francis Schaeffer, 1981, pp. 56. Used by permission of Crossway, a publishing ministry of Good News Publishers, Wheaton, IL 60187, www.crossway.org.

Appendix

Recommended Reading

Douglas A. Abbott & A. Dean Byrd, *Encouraging Heterosexuality* (Brigham Distributing 2009).

Alan Chambers, *God's Grace and The Homosexual Next Door: Reaching the Heart of the Gay Men and Woman in Your World* (Harvest House Publishers 2006).

Alan Chambers, *Leaving Homosexuality: A Practical Guide for Men and Woman Looking for a Way Out* (Harvest House Publishers 2009).

Joe Dallas, *The Gay Gospel? How Pro-Gay Advocates Misread the Bible* (Harvest House Publishers 2007).

Joe Dallas, *Desires in Conflict: Hope for Men Who Struggle with Sexual Identity* (Harvest House Publishers 2003).

Joe Dallas & Nancy Heche, *The Complete Christian Guide to Understanding Homosexuality* (Harvest House 2010).

Bob Davies & Lori Rentzel, *Coming Out of Homosexuality: New Freedom for Men and Women* (InterVarsity Press 1994).

Arthur Goldberg, *Light in the Closet: Torah, Homosexuality and the Power to Change* (Red Heifer Press 2009).

Julie Harren Hamilton and Philip Henry, *Handbook of Therapy for Unwanted Homosexual Attractions* (Xulon Press 2009).

Nancy Heche, *The Truth Comes Out* (Regal Books 2006).

Jeanette Howard, *Out of Egypt: One Woman's Journey out of Lesbianism* (Monarch Books 2000).

Robert Knight, *Radical Rulers* (CRM 2010).

David Kupelian, *The Marketing of Evil: How Radicals, Elitists, and Pseudo-Experts Sell Us Corruption Disguised as Freedom* (WND Books 2005).

Erwin W. Lutzer, *6 Things You Need to Know About What's Really at Stake: The Truth About Same-Sex Marriage* (Zondervan 2004).

NARTH Publication, *What Research Shows: NARTH's Response to the APA Claims on Homosexuality, The Journal of Human Sexuality Vol. 1* (2009).

Joseph Nicolosi, *A Parent's Guide to Preventing Homosexuality* (InterVarsity Press 2002).

Joseph Nicolosi, *Reparative Therapy of Male Homosexuality* (Aronson 1997).

Anne Paulk, *Restoring Sexual Identity: Hope for Women Who Struggle with Same-Sex Attraction* (Harvest House Publishers 2003).

Mathew D. Staver, *Same-Sex Marriage: Putting Every Household at Risk* (Broadman and Holman 2004).

Dawn Stefanowicz, *Out From Under: The Impact of Homosexual Parenting* (Annotation Press 2007).

Debbie Thurman, *Post-Gay Post-Christian? Anatomy of a Cultural and Faith Identity Crisis* (Cedar House Publishers 2011).

Rogers H. Wright and Nicholas A. Cummings, *Destructive Trends in Mental Health: The Well-Intentioned Path to Harm* (Taylor & Francis Group 2005).

Website Resources

Liberty Counsel (lc.org)

OnlyOneMommy.com

American Association of Christian Counselors (aacc.net)

American Family Association (afa.net)

Americans For Truth About Homosexuality (aftah.com)

Concerned Women for America (cwfa.org)

Exodus International (exodusinternational.org)

Family Research Council (frc.org)

JONAH (jonahweb.org)

Mission America (missionamerica.com)

NARTH (narth.org)

PFOX (pfox.org)

About the Author

Rena M. Lindevaldsen, Esq.

Prior to joining Liberty University School of Law in 2006, Rena Linde-valdsen served as Senior Litigation Counsel to Liberty Counsel, a non-profit litigation and education organization dedicated to advancing religious freedom, the sanctity of human life, and traditional family. She presently serves as Special Counsel to Liberty Counsel.

During her work with Liberty Counsel, she has been actively involved in efforts throughout the country to preserve traditional marriage through litigation, legislation, and constitutional amendments. She filed the first lawsuit to enjoin San Francisco's efforts to "marry" same-sex couples, and obtained two orders enjoining public officials in New York from officiating same-sex unions. She successfully challenged New York City's decision to publicly fund a high school for homosexual students and a Maryland school board's decision to implement sex education curriculum that presented materials hostile to conservative religious beliefs. For six years she was part of the legal team defending Lisa Miller.

Rena Lindevaldsen has appeared on numerous radio and television programs around the world and has been a speaker and panelist at a number of conferences, seminars, and debates around the country.

To learn more, visit Rena's blog at www.OnlyOneMommy.com.

CPSIA information can be obtained at www.ICGtesting.com
Printed in the USA
239641LV00004B/3/P